RALLYING!

TONY MASON & STUART TURNER

Foulis

Haynes

A FOULIS Motoring Book

First published 1988
Revised 1991
© Tony Mason and Stuart Turner
Haynes Publishing Group.

Published by:
Haynes Publishing Group
Sparkford, Nr. Yeovil,
Somerset BA22 7JJ, England

Haynes Publications Inc.
861 Lawrence Drive, Newbury Park,
California 91320 USA

**British Library Cataloguing in
Publication Data**

A catalogue record for this book is available
from the British Library

ISBN 0-85429-887-8

Library of Congress Catalog Card No.
91-72999

Editors: Robert Iles and Peter Nicholson
Design: Phil Lyons

Printed in England by: J.H. Haynes & Co.
Ltd

Typeset in Rockwell Light Condensed 11/12pt

CONTENTS

Walter Mitty in them to dream of winning the Open. Similarly when things are going well and a car is flowing over a special stage, lots of rally drivers must think that, given the breaks, they could be up there scrapping with the best of them. So they could; if they show enough application and determination. Even if you don't want to become a top line professional rally driver but only do the sport for fun, then you will still get more enjoyment out of your hobby if you go about it in the right way – by getting the right equipment, by studying your driving technique; by preparing your car properly, by going about your search for sponsorship in a businesslike way and by tackling the right rallies, in the right order.

In other words, by doing all the things which we hope this book will teach you.■

THE HISTORY

Rally drivers rarely stop to consider the history of their sport, preferring, rightly, to concentrate on preparations for their next event. Nevertheless, rallying has a long and reasonably noble history and it is worth taking a quick glance at that history here.

Purists may disagree but really the very first motoring events – such as the Paris to Rouen in 1894 and the Paris-Bordeaux-Paris in 1895 – were rallies, even though they were called races or reliability trials. They were rallies, because in those early days of motoring the challenge of actually getting to a place was one of the main incentives, the time taken or the overall position being secondary.

Cars in those events back at the turn of the century carried passengers, just like the modern rally cars; they were set off at intervals, just like modern rally cars, and there was a certain amount of navigation or route finding involved, again just as on many modern rallies. The main difference of course was that in those days there was more excitement in motoring; more of a sense of pioneering. Not so today, when at any moment parking seems likely to be made a capital offence.

Although France staged the first motor sport events, we must turn to Germany for the next milestone in any history of rallying because in 1904 Germany saw the Herkomer Trophy, which was a long distance regularity contest for touring cars. Competitors had to maintain strict average speeds between controls, which had to be visited in the right order. Sadly, the regulations were too complex and the rally finished in a flurry of arguments. One thing has thus remained constant throughout the history of rallying – if organisers try to be too clever, competitors will either try to find a way round the regulations or bitch about the results at the finish! All organisers should have a sign on their desks saying "Our job is to provide enjoyment for drivers".

Anyway, getting back to Germany, the Herkomer Trophy faded after a few years but the "Prinz Heinrich Fahrt" took its place. To their everlasting credit, the Imperial Automobile Club persuaded Prince Heinrich of Prussia to put his name to their event – and bear in mind that this was at a time when Germany had just introduced a car tax and speed limits.

The Automobile Club had 130 starters for their first event in 1908, including a couple of fellows not without connections with the motor industry – Bugatti and Opel. After seven days and 14,000 miles the winner was Fritz Erle in a Benz.

The rally spurred the Austrians into organising something similar and their Internationale Alpenfahrt started in 1910. The event grew in stature and by 1914 was attracting entries from all over Europe, including Rolls-Royce. By this time, incidentally, the name Audi had made an appearance in motor sport – winning the Transalpine Rally in 1913.

While the Germans and Austrians were busy building up their events, further south businessmen in Monte Carlo had watched the increasing popularity of the motor car and considered that an event in January

Early motor races and reliability trials could really be considered as rallies. The winner of the Paris-Bordeaux-Paris event in 189[ ] took two days and averaged 15 mph. Perhaps the cyclist was acting as service crew!

might help fill their hotels at a slack period. So a major milestone in rallying took place with the first Monte Carlo Rally in 1911. The organiser's sensible aim was to get as many people to Monte Carlo as possible and it was much less challenging than the event we know today. Nevertheless some of the elements of today's rally were there, with cars starting from several starting points throughout Europe.

After a disastrous Monte in 1924, when they switched to March, the rally really took hold from 1925 and during the Thirties regularly had over 150 starters. Perhaps January has always been a slow news month for sport – and there are worse places to be in the winter than Monte Carlo – as a result the event has always had wide media attention and even today is probably the best known motoring event in Europe.

Perhaps the most important year for British rally enthusiasts was 1929 because that was when the R.A.C. Rally started, although as it was a fairly gentle tour with just a few driving tests, it bore little resemblance to today's thrash through the forests.

Two years later, in 1931, the Royal Motor Union of Liège ran their first Marathon de la Route. The organisers were firm believers in 'no nonsense' rallies with the challenge coming from long and difficult routes, not from nit-picking regulations. In 1951 the

event became the Liège-Rome-Liège, then when roads became too crowded over that route, they switched in 1956 to Liège-Sofia-Liège. If you want to see grown men cry, mention "The Liège" to any of the ageing rally stars who once were lucky enough to do it. The sheer challenge of around ninety hours of virtually non-stop motoring over dusty roads in Yugoslavia and Bulgaria was quite something.

An almost standard Standard on a 1959 Monte Carlo Rally. Roof mounted spotlights are now banned. Note the outside horns!

Occasionally the organisers would be asked by the authorities to put in 'secret checks'. They would solemnly announce this at the drivers' briefing then hold up a card on which, surprise, surprise, was written the location of the checks!

The other 'classic' which deserves an honourable mention in any history is the Alpine, or to give it is full title "The Coupe des Alpes". This started in 1949 and through to its demise in the early 1970s provided a tough menu of special sections over mountain passes – so much so that a 'Coupe' for a penalty free run rightly became the most cherished prize in the sport. A 'Gold' Coupe for three Coupes in consecutive years was roughly equivalent to three Olympic Gold Medals.

The late 1950s saw a gradual but positive shift among competitors from amateur to professional (in attitude if not earning power) or if you like, from gentlemen to players. Happily it happened without any interference from promoters. The sport has always been free of squabbles over amateurs and professionals, possibly because it has always been so expensive that even the wealthy competitors have been glad to accept help! We are not suggesting that rally drivers before the Fifties were not serious, obviously they were, but the new breed were virtually full-time professionals earning their living at the sport and therefore able to spend a lot of time practising.

The second big change seen in the late Fifties was the start of the Scandinavian invasion. Eric Carlsson was the pioneering angel and his exploits with the Saab became legendary – "The biggest driver in the smallest car" was a journalist's dream.

Rauno Aaltonen was one of the next Scandinavians to make an impact (arriving from a co-driver's seat in the Mercedes team) and then of course they came in hordes.

No-one has really explained why; perhaps the roads in Sweden and Finland give them plenty of opportunity to practise; perhaps the long dark nights do something to the soul which makes good rally drivers. Whatever it is (and if you could bottle it you could make a fortune) you have to accept that, the Scandinavians have produced a disproportionate number of rally stars for their population, although there are signs that the Latin countries are now where the future heroes are likely to come from; just as Borg encouraged other Swedes to take tennis seriously, so Carlos Sainz is likely to be followed by other Spanish rally stars.

If we jump forward ten years to the late

Stirling Moss won a coveted Gold Cup in a Sunbeam on the Alpine Rally in 1954. He was a brilliant driver in both races and rallies – one of the very few to succeed in both.

One of the classic rally cars – the Austin-Healey 3000 seen here on Mont Ventoux on the 1962 Alpine Rally. Cars of this era are now being seen in action again with a number of rallies organised for them.

Leader of the Scandanavian invasion Eric Carlsson comes up to a standing ovation with his Saab after his first R.A.C. Rally win.

Paddy Hopkirk's Mini-Cooper 'S' on its way to an historic win in the Monte Carlo Rally back in 1964. He remains one of the best known British rally drivers.

Andrew Cowan winning the 1977 London to Sydney Rally in a Mercedes-Benz – nine years after he won the first in a Hillman Hunter.

A major turning point in rallying came in the early eighties when Audi developed their four wheel drive Quattro. This is Michèle Mouton on the Acropolis Rally.

One of the world's longest rallies – the 1970 London to Mexico 'World Cup' – won by the Ford Escort of Hannu Mikkola and Gunnar Palm. The Escort became another classic rally car with wins all over the world.

The Metro 6R4 entered international rallying in 1985 and captured the British public's imagination. Sadly, despite a couple of high placings on the Lombard RAC Rally in the hands of Tony Pond, it failed to emulate its famous predecessor – the Mini.

Sixties we see perhaps the greatest change in our history – the growth of sponsorship. Rallying became perhaps more democratic and as youngsters with more ability than cash fought to reach the top, they naturally turned to sponsors to lubricate their efforts. Companies like Castrol and Shell and others had long supported people in racing and rallying but they realised that they would get better value if more people were aware of their involvement – hence the sponsor's decal (or sticker). Later, cars appeared in properly planned total colour schemes.

With the advent of sponsors – particularly those from non-motoring areas who brought in fresh ideas – came professional public relations and better media coverage. Rallying still doesn't receive the media attention it perhaps deserves, either on television or in the national press,

though what there is gets increasingly international with Swedish TV covering the Safari, Spanish TV covering the Lombard R.A.C. Rally and so on. All good stuff for manufacturers and sponsors.

Other historical milestones? The growth of stage events at the expense of "road" rallies (that is events on public roads in which navigation plays a significant part) in Britain – inevitable with faster cars, but still sad. Apart from anything else road rallies provide a great training ground, not just in disciplining a crew but also in finding people to become involved in team management because the need for attention to detail in the two areas is very similar.

But enough history. We will try to forecast what the *future* holds for rallying in the last chapter of this book but now let us move on to the next chapter and look at the different sorts of rallies you can tackle. ▪

TYPES OF RALLY

Although no two rallies are exactly alike, it is possible to place them in certain categories; at one end of the scale the small club social rally and at the other the glamorous, rugged full-blown International. Each type has its own specialists, its own fans and its own champions. The various types require different skills from competitors and perhaps the only constant factor is that a reliable car of some sort is needed for success – speed and performance being less critical on many events.

You will need a car, driver and co-driver/navigator/passenger for any rally, although the ratio of importance of the two members of the crew will vary according to the event. On a club rally where there are numerous navigational problems, the responsibility for success falls fairly and squarely on the navigator; as long as the driver can operate the controls of the car there is no reason why he should not chauffeur his able colleague to victory.

It is also possible for an unbalanced crew to win another type of rally altogether – a good special stage driver can frequently win a very simple stage rally even if accompanied by a very simple co-driver!

However these are the extremes and the basic recipe for success in rallying is a good combination of crew talents plus a reliable vehicle, one prepared with care and attention to detail.

There are two types of rally in Britain. One is the road rally where the car and crew are required to pass given points at specified times and spend the entire period of the rally on public roads. Naturally a restriction on the maximum required average speed is imposed to avoid racing on the public highway or exceeding statutory speed limits. The other is the stage rally which we shall come to later.

Let's now look at the different types of event, starting in the lower echelons and working up to the world-famous rallies. We hope devotees of the car treasure hunt will forgive us if we start with their particular event which is often regarded as the lowest end of the scale.

Road events

Many clubs and societies like to run car treasure hunts as part of their social calendar, however most countries have regulations controlling the running of events on public highways and Britain is no exception. It is against the law to run on the public highway any unauthorised motoring event of more than twelve cars wherein the driver may receive any form of time penalty. Therefore, organisers of treasure hunts can break the law unless they take care. Nevertheless it is still possible to organise successful treasure hunts which stay well within the law, yet provide innocent entertainment for the participants.

Treasure hunts tend to take place in daylight hours and the basic requirement is to solve clues or gather pieces of information as the car travels round a gentle route. The route itself may be given by clues and questions; some organisers lay

Only standard road cars can be used on road rallies. Notice no plates or racing numbers.

Road rallies are still very popular for clubmen.

on a mobile *Times* crossword, others prefer a more lighthearted approach. Whatever the style of event, it must be organised with care and competitors should not need to leave their cars to record answers. They can be good fun and provide good mental exercise – all good navigator training.

Despite the social nature of the treasure hunt, prospective organisers should advise the police of the passage of the event. Great care must, of course, be taken with the use of narrow lanes in the route.

The only rallies which do not require full authorisation from the Royal Automobile Club Motor Sports Association Ltd. (who act on behalf of the Department of the Environment) are those in which twelve cars or less compete. Even so, these events are subject to some restrictions and organisers must advise the police and the RACMSA of any event that is planned. These events cannot take the form of straightforward competitive road events.

The organisation of a twelve car rally is obviously much easier than a bigger one, and such events are popular with motor clubs who frequently run them as training events for less experienced members. As

they are usually run to the rigid rules of the bigger events, they make a good starting point for the raw beginner. They are often short in distance and will probably take place during an evening. Like most road events, it is advisable to run them during darkness as the narrow lanes of Britain are less than ideal for safe competition motoring in daylight hours.

Moving on from twelve-car events, we come to the 'closed-to-club' rally. This event will be organised to conform to all the rules and regulations applying to any major road rally; the route will have to be authorised in detail but participation in the event will be restricted to members of the promoting club only. The mileage will probably not be very great but neither will the expense of competing (nor the awards for that matter!). It is not necessary to have an RACMSA competition licence in order to compete in a 'closed-to-club' rally; all you need is a Club membership card. The next stage up is the 'Clubman eight' event, confined to members of not more than eight clubs.

Moving up the scale, probably the most popular grade of rally is the 'Restricted/Regional' club rally. Here a club will extend an invitation to other neighbouring or prominent motor clubs (usually up to a maximum of fifteen) whose members will be entitled to compete in the event upon production of a current club membership card plus the competition licence of the appropriate grade.

Noise level is an important factor in the case of all road rallies and cars are scrutineered before the start of any event. Should an exhaust system be damaged or develop a fault during an event, the crew will probably find themselves penalised or excluded by noise marshals who lurk in the lanes.

Road rallies up to Restricted/Regional level may have the routes defined by map references or more intricate methods. Either way, the navigator will play an important role. On a really difficult navigational event the person in the passenger seat plays by far the more important part. Most of the route will confine itself to lanes and byways, some non-surfaced and occasionally non-charted. Some sections, on more deserted parts of the route, may be timed to the second but there are restrictions on the number of 'selective' sections allowed. 'Selectives', by the way, should only be run after midnight. Maps will be of great importance and almost certainly the excellent Ordnance Survey maps will be used.

There are now very few road rally championships and the RACMSA have laid down strict regulations to control this section of the sport. Clocks must be set to BBC time (thus preventing organisers being tempted to tighten times of sections by adjusting clocks) and a strict 30 mph average is a legal requirement. More difficult navigation is now normal and map references and other navigational instructions will, almost always, have to be dealt with on the move; it used to be common for these to be handed to navigators well before the start. In other words, any events which use the public highway should be navigational exercises and flat-out driving by rally cars should be restricted to special stage events on private land.

Incidentally one area of training for navigators which, for some reason, is rarely mentioned in motoring circles is the sport of orienteering. Orienteers are required to visit various points on a map – on foot by the way – covering different types of terrain, reaching the finish within a specified time. Rallying and orienteering both have a fanatical following in Scandina-

's possible to use a standard, unsponsored 'road ar' on stages but rougher vents should be avoided.

via and the whole question of map reading, course plotting and "reading the countryside" is common to both. The only difference is that the orienteering map reader does not need a car or driver. No one would seriously describe orienteering as a type of car rally but as a navigational training exercise it is worth more than a passing thought. Many drivers are far from physically fit – maybe they, too, could benefit from a spot of orienteering!

Stage events

Now let's look at the other type of event is the special stage rally where cars enjoy relatively easy public road sections but are required to cover stages on private land at high speeds. It is very much a 'Jekyll and Hyde' operation as drivers have to cope with gentle road sections then fierce and fast stages. The stages can be found on private farm tracks, disused airfields and railway lines or in the magnificent forest tracks of Britain. Enterprising organisers have been known to use private roads in stately homes, factories, the roads around sewerage plants, and believe it or not, the subterranean tracks of a coalmine. The last named was featured in a Swedish rally many moons ago, but then there are no bounds to the imagination of rally organisers in Sweden and Finland. Scandinavian rally stages frequently traverse frozen lakes and rivers, sometimes with the stage carved out of the snow on a lake's frozen surface by a snow plough a few hours before the cars are due.

British stages can be muddy, rocky and rough, but are very popular with competitors despite the higher costs of competing on a stage rally rather than a road event, because of the greater likelihood of damage to the car.

Stage events, like road rallies are very popular at Restricted grade and usually last one full day or one full night rather than the half day or half night of lesser events.

Stage rallies operate at all grades in Britain, the Restricted/Regional grade being by far the most common. Many of these rallies have access to the wide variety of loose surface tracks in Britain's forests, although the Forestry Commission has stringent rules about the amount of use each road may have, as well as on the charges to be levied on organisers and routes to be taken. However without the use of these tracks the British rally scene would be a lot poorer and have far less capable drivers in its ranks.

As Restricted/Regional rallies are run to RACMSA regulations it is necessary for competing cars to conform to all the requirements laid down by the RACMSA, so they will have to pass the inspection of a Scrutineer before the event starts. Stage and road events have different requirements but all relate to safety, be it the safety of competitors or that of spectators.

The level of crew responsibility changes in the case of stage rallies, the driver assuming a far more important role. The car must be tough and well prepared, and will need greater performance than its road rally counterpart. Tyre patterns and compounds become more important and conversation turns to differentials, cams, special driveshafts, six-speed gearboxes and the like.

Total stage mileage can range from 25 to a hundred miles or more and the road mileage can be literally anything; it will probably consist of main road or even motorway driving at times, all totally non-competitive. Single venue events are also popular; here the competing cars attempt several stages within a large park, quarry or disused airfield and run to full rally regulations but never venture onto the public road which, of course, makes the organisers' lot a little easier. The same stage may often be used twice or more.

On a stage rally the pressure is really on the driver to drive as quickly as possible from the start of each stage to the finish. The length of the stages varies from a mere mile or two to twenty miles or more, although anything above twenty is rare. Organisers usually place prominent arrows at junctions and bends, and mark hazard spots on the track and in the road book; start and finish points are clearly marked by large boards, too. The navigator, who is starting to assume the role of co-driver (we shall discuss the delicate terminology later) has to keep an eye on the whole proceedings, though he won't have to find the route from the map (although some co-drivers on British events find that following maps of forests helps their driver considerably). Maps are allowed and even encouraged but markings on these maps are limited by regulations – some organisers even supply copies of 1:25000 maps in the roadbook. Most importantly; the co-driver will keep an eye on the stage and help confirm arrows to his driver. He will tell him how far it is to the finish in the event of a puncture or other problem so that the driver can decide whether to stop or limp on, and he will check the time carefully on arrival at the finish of a stage. There are stage target times, times of arrival and departure at stages, fuel halts, road controls, etc., to think about so the co-driver is kept carefully occupied.

National special stage rallies have a minimum stage total of fifty miles (75 miles in the case of National Championship events) and are open to any national competition licence holder. They tend to concentrate on forestry roads and consist entirely of special stages. These full day or full night events usually attract a good entry of well-prepared cars, all of which conform to the regulations stipulated for a national event. The rallies take place in all parts of the United Kingdom and usually qualify for a major championship.

There are a number of British International forest rallies – other than the famed Lombard R.A.C. – and it is the aim of many Clubmen to compete in one of these events during their rally careers. Using the best of the forest tracks available to them, these rallies enjoy a high standard of organi-

The Manx International is all tarmac and very fast – as James Cullen and Ellen Morgan demonstrate.

There are class awards on most rallies, the 'up to 1300 cc' being among the most hotly contested.

Finland isn't the only rally with 'yumps'. This is Portugal.

Most World Championship rallies feature 'Super Special Stages' to entertain the crowds. Erwin Weber's VW Golf performs before a full house on the Rally of Portugal.

sation, and often attract some top overseas drivers, so giving Britons the taste of International rally conditions. The Welsh and Scottish Rallies are by far the best known of these: British works and dealer teams and overseas works teams enter these events, giving them a reasonably international flavour.

The pinnacle in Britain is of course the Lombard R.A.C. Since its move to the forests thirty years ago the rally has gone from strength to strength and now enjoys the healthiest entry list of any rally in the world. Many of the top drivers rate it as one of their favourite events. It has become firmly established as a major spectator and sporting event in Britain and over two million people turn out to watch the five day rally each year; the TV programmes attract large audiences, there is regular radio coverage and there are big sales of video tapes.

Before leaving the British scene, mention must be made of the very popular and extremely demanding tarmac stage rallies. Thanks to the favourable views of their governments to closing public roads, Ireland and the Isle of Man provide opportunities for British drivers to gain the

sort of experience once only available to Continentals. Ireland boasts the Easter weekend Circuit of Ireland, as well as the Ulster, Donegal, Galway and other rallies and the Isle of Man produces the Manx International and the shorter Manx Stages each year. The events are pure stage rallies and most cars run on racing tyres and even lowered suspension. Events last two or three days, and thanks to the high speeds and unforgiving bumps, often have fewer finishers than any forest rally of comparable length. A small tarmac stage rally in the holiday Channel Island of Jersey is also in the British Calendar.

World rallying

Mainland Europe still plays host to the World Rally Circus for much of the rally year and there are numerous other major events held in the classic mountains of Europe, and very demanding they are too. Some British club drivers make sorties to compete in these European events, particularly the small International rallies in Spain, Portugal or Southern France, as these can be combined with a holiday.

The world of rallying has spread its

Mike Kirkland and Robin Nixon hurry across the plains of Kenya in a Nissan 200SX. African Rallies are always spectacular and demanding.

David Llewellin on the Scottish Rally – one of the roughest forest events in Britain.

wings and there are major events in every corner of the world. Large countries with sparse populations permit long, fast open road sections, and on African rallies, cars can go for hours without ever touching an asphalt road.

Developing countries are keen to add rallying to their list of attractions and the African and Middle Eastern countries have numerous events and their own championships.

Rallying is slowly becoming more popular in the United States of America and that country appears to be moving well away from the 'navigational nightmares' of the Seventies.

There are also numerous rallies in the Eastern bloc countries and the U.S.S.R.

sends its State Rally Team on periodic sorties outside the Soviet Union. Czechoslovakia in particular regards rallying very highly and their Skoda team is renowned for scooping class awards on many events all over the world.

Rallying is rapidly gaining in popularity in the Far East and an Asian Pacific Championship includes rounds in Malaysia, Indonesia, India and Thailand. Small rallies are run in Hong Kong, believe it or not. Rallying continues in overpopulated Japan

Rallying is popular in Eastern European countries. Skoda have had an amazingly long run of class successes on the Lombard R.A.C. Rally.

A forest is a forest is a forest . . . ! Carlos Sainz feels quite at home on the other side of the world in the New Zealand Rally.

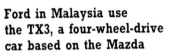

Ford in Malaysia use
the TX3, a four-wheel-drive
car based on the Mazda

Five times Australian
Champion Ross Dunkerton
tackles the rocky roads
down-under on the Wynns
Safari.

although most of the rallies there are of a navigational nature, owing to the type of terrain and the laws of the land.

Australia is noted for its rugged style of events but now hosts one of the best World Championship rounds, a forest event based on Perth. New Zealand also has a strong rallying fraternity with 'European-style' events and several South American countries produce rallies of varying types, Argentina

usually hosting a World Championship event.

So, regardless of politics, petrol prices, creed or colour, there are rallies in every corner of the world. There are rallies on tiny islands in the Southern hemisphere, there are rallies hundreds of miles north of the Arctic circle, and, if that is not enough, there are trans-Sahara events like the much vaunted Paris-Dakar and even occasional trans-world marathons.

Toyota spearheaded the Japanese invasion of world rallying using the Toyota Celica GT4.

Marathons like the Paris-Dakar event are open to every type of vehicle from motorcycles to trucks. Bjorn Waldegard and Fred Gallagher kick up the dust in their Citroën.

HOW & WHERE TO START

The simplest way to get the flavour of rallying is as a *spectator*. If you take this route, do remember that spectators cause more complaints from the public than rally competitors, so:-

DO
- drive sensibly
- obey marshals' instructions
- park where directed
- arrive at stages early and be prepared for long walks into the forests
- watch out for flying stones (a rally car at speed can hurl them like bullets)
- keep well back from the rally road
- be prepared to pay on major events like the Lombard R.A.C.

DON'T
- leave litter
- drive like a maniac on public roads
- stand in silly places
- smoke in forest areas or where a car is being serviced
- take a dog with you

All commonsense points but they are not always observed!

If spectating whets your appetite then the next level of involvement is *marshalling*. This takes you closer to the action and organisers will welcome your services with open arms, BUT, marshalling brings with it responsibilities – don't *just* treat it as a way of getting closer to the action. Above all you must be reliable and responsible and you must follow the organisers' instructions. Don't be officious – rallying should be fun for all concerned.

Motor clubs

If having marshalled, you want to take up rallying as a *competitor*, the first thing to do is to join a motor club which is recognised by the R.A.C. To obtain recognition a club has to be reasonably well established and must operate in accordance with rules drawn up by the R.A.C. There are over eight hundred recognised clubs in Britain and apart from providing a starting point for budding drivers and navigators they also offer a good social side.

The R.A.C. Motor Sports Association Ltd., Motor Sports House, Riverside Park, Colnbrook, Slough, SL3 OHG (Telephone 0753 681 736, Fax 0753 682938, Telex 847796 Racing G) will be able to supply a list of clubs in your area or, better still, you should buy a copy of their *Year Book* which includes addresses of all motor clubs as well as a lot of other useful information.

Most clubs have a leaning towards one particular branch of the sport so if there are several in your area write to the secretaries to find out their main interests – as a budding rally driver it would make no sense to join a club specialising in hillclimbing.

Later in your rally career you will almost certainly join more than one club, including one of the better rally clubs so that you get invitations to the best rallies.

There are a handful of national clubs like the British Trial and Rally Drivers Association but most clubs are based in one

Colin McRae started rallying at club level in a Vauxhall Nova before
graduating to more powerful cars.

particular locality and are linked with other clubs in their area to form Regional Associations of the RACMSA.

It is pretty certain that you will find a motor club based in your nearest town, so join it.

Each year the average motor club organises, or co-organises with neighbouring clubs, a handful of road and stage rallies of a "Closed-to-club" status and possibly one major Restricted rally as well; in addition it probably organises some twelve-car rallies. It will almost certainly hold regular club meetings, film shows and social functions.

Driving

It is obviously wise to decide at an early stage if you wish to concentrate on driving or navigating although a dabble at both is an excellent thing before you get too serious. At this early stage, the potential driver need not have the latest specification of rally car (nor will he need to worry about the ramifications of 'homologation'). In fact, it's a positive disadvantage to possess a highly tuned vehicle for it could be dangerous if the capability of the car is way ahead of his skills. Better to start with a modest vehicle and work up to the faster machinery.

The legendary Roger Clark started rallying in a Ford 5 cwt. van while Russell Brookes borrowed an Austin Westminster before he graduated to a Morris Minor 1000 of his own. Hannu Mikkola started on the road to super-stardom on local events in Finland in a secondhand Volvo PV 544. There are other stars, who used to borrow their company car for innocent events but we would not recommend this to anyone who hopes to get a gold watch for long service with their company!

The point we are making is that any type of car will be acceptable at these early stages and whatever the performance of the car you will soon see if you, as a driver or navigator, have any desire to progress to greater things.

A driver should simply see that the car is mechanically sound, has good underbody protection, good lights and tyres and, of course, good brakes. Obviously an experi-

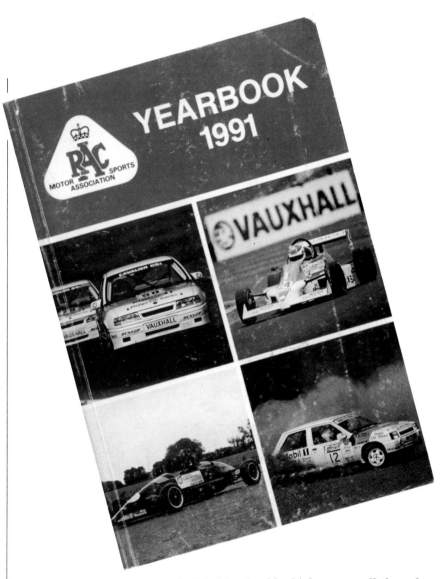

Essential reading – the RACMSA 'blue book' which covers all the rules, regulations and fixtures for British motorsports.

enced navigator can be an enormous help to a driver but it must be made quite clear that the driver is hoping to *learn* from his early events, he should not try to impress the experienced partner with great heroics.

Navigating

The navigator's beginning will be very similar to the driver's although his major investment will be a few pencils, one or two simple navigational instruments and an Ordnance Survey map or two. The problem of pairing is very much the same as the driver's – don't select a very experienced driver (if he'll have you) as you'll be so frightened of making a mistake that you will probably make one within a mile of the start.

Be completely honest with your partner and preferably learn together.

Many successful navigators started rallying at tender ages, among them are Arne Hertz, Fred Gallagher and Ian Grindrod. Mike Broad, who navigated the winning car on the last London-Sydney rally, competed in his first event at fourteen. Some navigators start before they can drive a car and many do not even possess a car – we mention this because some people think that they cannot join a car club if they do not own a car. Not so! A navigator is fortunate because it will not cost a lot of money to practise.

Grasp every opportunity to compete on a rally, no matter how small. Practise map reference plotting and practise more difficult navigational exercises too. Get hold of old route cards from previous rallies and go through them.

Some navigators have been known to sit in a darkened room in a rocking chair holding a torch, plotting map references under simulated rally car conditions. It's not a bad idea! If you can persuade a friend to take you for short drives, do so, and read the map while you go. You can follow a prescribed route from an old route card or even a route you have devised yourself. Try a few 'table top rallies' – motor clubs often run these as social evenings. Above all, gain every bit of experience you can – practise, practise, practise.

Practice

While budding navigators are gaining as much map experience as possible, the driver should be concentrating on building up experience in the driving seat. Drive on as many events as you can. Don't worry if your car is unsuitable for the event in question, don't worry if you cannot win – just keep piling up those vital hours of experience. Loose surface auto-tests are always good and several clubs organise events of this nature. You may say that dodging plastic pylons is not what you aim to do for the rest of your motor sport career – don't worry, just think of the pylon as a fir tree or gatepost. There'll come a time when you'll be glad of that pylon dodging practise.

Many top drivers have spent time gaining racing experience in their early careers while some found rallycross good training for developing judgement, timing and car control.

Practise driving under all conditions. Don't go berserk racing around the lanes but do go for long drives on deserted tracks in adverse weather conditions. If there is snow or fog – get out and practise. You'll be surprised how these two elements can alter rally results.

Many top drivers started driving at a very early age; some of those brought up in a motoring environment were capable drivers by the time they were ten years old! Needless to say, they only practised on private tracks or in fields.

Whatever your age or background the message is clear; drive, drive! Please do not trespass when practising your driving. Do not, ever, try to get onto Forestry Commission land or any private land; this will not only spoil your training plans if you are caught but, much more important, it will have a damaging effect on rally relations with land owners.

Remember that a good rally driver needs a combination of talents. He should have good balance, extremely good judgement, good reactions and good timing. The Americans have an apt saying to describe the cause of many motor sport accidents. "It was the right foot in the wrong place".

Speaking of balance, you may find motor cycle experience helpful. Pentti Airikkala and Jimmy McRae swear that it was trail riding that helped them hone their driving skill. Alex Fiorio was Italian junior downhill ski champion and attributes his car control to that while Carlos Sainz succeeded in other sports before conquering rallying.

All the top rally crews are strong believers in personal fitness and most of them are strictly tee-total and non-smokers; some even keep strictly to specially designed diets. All too much like hard work? Then accept you will never reach the top and simply rally for fun.

Although it is useful to try rallies with different partners, there is no doubt that you are likely to have more success if you develop a permanent partnership. It is

One-make championships are an excellent place to start; the Peugeot GTI club being particularly successful.

important to develop a rapport with your partner particularly if you intend to compete in road rallies because the best road rally crews will almost be able to read each other's minds. A driver will understand instructions merely by the intonation in the navigator's voice when giving an instruction. Similarly, a navigator will be able to forestall a driver's question about the distance to petrol, or the penalty marks to date. A driver must be kept supplied with appropriate information (not too much trivia) although they do have an annoying habit of asking for it at the most inconvenient moments.

In stage rallies a good partnership is also an advantage and when one starts to use pace notes the degree of trust and rapport which exist between the crew can be vital.

One of the problems encountered by the navigator in the early stages of map reading may be the dreaded travel sickness. Don't be put off by this rather unpleasant problem. Remember that many of today's top co-drivers have been sick at some time or other and travel sickness is usually overcome by confidence: confidence in your driver, confidence in your ability and confidence in your stomach. However, it will be wise to take one or two precautions at an early stage. Although some of the more experienced co-drivers eat copious supplies of fattening, filling food before an event (they work on the principle that they never know when it might be their last meal!) it is wise to eat sensible amounts of non-greasy foods before a rally. Naturally it would be irresponsible for either crew member to consider taking any alcohol. Don't starve yourself completely – you will not work accurately or efficiently if you are suffering from hunger pangs.

One of the major causes of travel sickness is the constant change in length of vision for the navigator – from the map to the road ahead and vice-versa. To avoid this, try to keep the knees which support the map-board as high as possible so that

your eyes do not have to glance too far up and down when reading the map or when looking out of the windscreen – probably 50% of your time will be devoted to each. The other precaution is to have full harness seat belts *fastened as tightly as possible*. This keeps you at one with the car and although you might feel as though you are being shaken to pieces, you will find less of a sickening problem.

Ian Grindrod suffered badly from sickness when he first started rallying (as a child he had been unable to travel for two miles on a bus without the inevitable happening) and he regarded the travel sickness problems as the greatest mental barrier to be overcome. He claims that confidence in one's own ability lessens the problem by fifty percent and after he had won his first small award he was never sick again! Many other top co-drivers had similar experiences.

Another tip from the top co-drivers is to

Winning lady! Louise Aitken-Walker was the winner of Ford's 'find a lady rally driver' competition and went on to become Britain's first ever winner of a World Rally title – that of Ladies World Rally Champion. She also beat most of the men she encountered!

This is Timo Salonen's Mazda 323 on the Swedish Rally.

practise reading anything you can lay your hands on when travelling in a car. You might be accused of being anti-social if you sit with your nose buried in a book when riding as a passenger in a car but it can help your problem.

If you really have a sickness problem and don't seem able to cure it, see your doctor, but make sure you tell him about your navigational activities as some of the stronger travel drugs (only available on prescription) have a very strong drowsiness effect.

Both crew members should read as much about rallying as they can (there are lots of starving rally writers about – they all need your help). Go to rally film and video shows, listen and ask questions when your local club has an expert competitor as a guest speaker. Go to forums to listen and ask – you'll be surprised what you can learn. Even a fellow panelist learned a new car control trick after listening to one of Hannu Mikkola's answers on a rally forum some years ago.

In this age of high video technology and sophisticated show business techniques, the beginner has many opportunities to see and hear a great deal about rallying and to meet top crews as the sport's major

sponsors put on rally shows for the clubs. Never miss one!

A driver can also learn useful technical tips from these shows and from lectures, forums and discussions, and he should certainly be reading as much as he can about rally preparation. Although some drivers are not particularly mechanically-minded, it is an advantage for the driver to have some mechanical knowledge. If he gets into a works team he will need such knowledge in order to be able to communicate with the engineers.

A navigator usually has no interest whatsoever in the mechanics of a car, but it is again not a bad thing to have some basic knowledge. However your career develops and however many service crews you will employ, you'll still need to do your own running repairs from time to time.

Talking of service, you'll probably decide to take a service crew along when you do stage events (though only, repeat only, if permitted by the regulations). This may well be necessary if only to change wheels if you're lucky enough to have a choice of tyres. The service crew might simply be a friend in a car with a few tools and spares in the boot or an estate car/van overflowing with parts and equipment. Either way, someone is going to have to pay.

Expense

Some club members will be delighted to act as a service crew and pay their own petrol or hotel costs as it is their way of enjoying the sport – others may need a contribution. One thing is certain, you'll need to work out costs in detail and be very clear about who pays what, long before the event. Good rally friendships have been ruined by financial misunderstandings.

While on the topic of money we should also explain that there is no hard and fast rule for sharing expenses. Rallying is an expensive pastime (which is why a later chapter is solely devoted to money matters) although the amount you spend depends on your level of participation. Basically, drivers are usually responsible for all the costs of car preparation, including parts, although it really depends on the personal financial situation of the competitors. It is not uncommon to share entry fees and running costs between navigator and driver, but on a stage event where the driver gains the greater kudos this may not be acceptable.

Whatever you decide, make sure it is cut and dried before you set off and also make sure who gets the prize money if any comes your way. However, as this chapter is about the beginner in motor sport, it is unlikely you'll see much prize money at this stage.

It is necessary for the driver to be absolutely sure his car is properly insured for any event and while on the subject of insurance we should mention life insurance. Many policies exclude dangerous sports and for insurance purposes a rally is considered a dangerous sport. Some insurance companies can include an endorsement which allows rallying to take place, so make sure that yours is one – if not, change; an insurance broker will probably give you the best advice – some specialise in motorsport. Although we do not wish to become too macabre, a brief word about wills might not go amiss. As the events you enter grow in size, so will the distances you travel and there are, regrettably, occasional deaths involving travel and motorsport. See your solicitor to make sure your affairs are in order.

PERSONAL EQUIPMENT

Safety and comfort are the two things to consider when choosing the first piece of personal equipment – clothing.

Top crews pay close attention to both matters and very expensive flame-resistant overalls, gloves, underwear and socks are the order of the day for them. If you are lucky enough to find yourself in this category you will be fully au fait with the latest, safest rally wear and more than likely your sponsor or team will pay for most of it! However, for lesser mortals the choice of clothing is still important.

Competitors on smaller road rallies will probably not need to go to the expense of purchasing overalls, but may simply wear jeans and pullover. Some drivers prefer 'shirt-sleeve order', others drive in a rally jacket with the car window open. Incidentally, drivers' window-opening habits should be borne in mind when navigators are planning their rallying wardrobe.

Footwear and gloves are again a matter of personal choice, but drivers' shoes should have no projections which might foul the pedals. Gloves should have chamois leather backs if you are likely to use them to clean the screen. Remember that whatever you wear, you're likely to find yourself scrambling under the car at some point so it's advisable not to wear your best suit.

A navigator on a road event may prefer to wear a jacket, or something with several pockets, it is necessary to carry erasers, spare pencils and other paraphenalia. He may also collect route-check cards and other bits of paper en route. Again, the latest Gucci footwear is not recommended for the navigator as he will probably find himself running along a ditch to a control at some time during a rally. Waterproof shoes are worth considering – in Canadian and Scandanavian winter rallies many co-drivers wear fur-lined boots with studded soles.

Rally overalls are, of course, widely worn by drivers and navigators and they certainly make sense. Being purpose-built they save other clothing, keep the body at the right temperature, and may even make the crew feel and perform better. Fire-proof overalls are recommended and come in varying grades. They are an obvious safety precaution, although they can be a trifle uncomfortable on hot long-distance events. If you buy such clothing make sure it meets the very latest international standards.

Colour and design of overalls are matters of personal choice, although light colours are safer; you may find yourself dancing around in a forest track, or changing a wheel, when another competitor comes along and you'll be seen more easily. Most overall manufacturers only produce one-piece suits. These are safer if the driver has to be pulled out of a car by outside helpers, although two-piece overalls seem more popular with rally crews. Remember that nylon must not be worn next to the skin.

Decorate your overalls with badges by all means, but try to keep a sense of neatness and decorum. Appearances are important and help the sport, so keep unnecessary and vulgar signs off your clothing. It's worth remembering that your

Buy the best equipment you can find. That includes fireproof overalls, gloves and a fully approved helmet.

most important decal (probably your sponsor's) should be as close to the chin as possible, as this is the one seen on photographs and film and television interviews. Some people embroider their blood group on their overalls; a sensible safety precaution but professional crews will also have this on a wrist bracelet or on a disc round their neck as, in the unhappy event of an accident, their overalls might not reach hospital with them.

Rally jackets come in a proliferation of sizes, colours and designs and if you are not lucky enough to be given one by your team or sponsor then choose a practical one. The co-driver's jacket should have pockets large enough to carry passports, licences and rally documents like time cards (the latter may have to be stored safely during waits at main rest halts or controls). Make sure the rally jacket has a built-in hood; many have fold away hoods and these are particularly suitable because there will be a cold, wet and windy night when you will welcome something to keep your head warm whilst waiting at a control or stage start (or when waiting for a breakdown truck!).

Helmets

Talking of headgear brings us on to safety helmets – an essential part of rally equipment on all but the smallest road rally. When selecting a crash helmet make sure you choose one that fits you properly. *A badly fitting crash helmet can be more dangerous than no helmet at all.* In any case, unless you feel comfortable you will not be able to function in the rally properly.

Sizes in different makes may vary. Make sure the helmet you select is not too tight and certainly not too slack. A driver on one Manx Rally found that everything had gone dark after one particularly ferocious hump; his helmet was far too big and had slipped over his eyes. Not the safest way to go rallying!

Helmets are expensive but remember you are protecting a vital part of your body.

Decide whether you wish to wear a full-face or open-face model. There's a price difference and some people find a slightly claustrophobic effect when wearing a full face, but they are safe and find an increasing use in rallying today. In some countries it is compulsory for both members of crew to wear full-face helmets. One word of caution, if you wear a fully enclosed helmet, make sure you can get an adequate supply of fresh air, otherwise you may perform below par simply through breathing stale air.

Whatever style or make of helmet you wear, make sure that your choice carries the latest 'approval' numbers and other

BS 6658 – 85 'A'
SNELL SA 85, M85

Crash helmet size chart

Size in inches (by tape measure)	$20\frac{1}{2}$	$20\frac{7}{8}$	$21\frac{1}{4}$	$21\frac{5}{8}$	22	$22\frac{1}{2}$	$22\frac{7}{8}$	$23\frac{1}{4}$	$23\frac{5}{8}$	24	$24\frac{3}{8}$
Hat size	$6\frac{3}{8}$	$6\frac{1}{2}$	$6\frac{5}{8}$	$6\frac{3}{4}$	$6\frac{7}{8}$	7	$7\frac{1}{8}$	$7\frac{1}{4}$	$7\frac{3}{8}$	$7\frac{1}{2}$	$7\frac{5}{8}$
Helmet size	Extra Small	Extra Small	S	S	M	M	L	L	Extra Large	Extra Large	Extra Large

Ready for action! Overalls, helmet, gloves, seat-belts and seats should all be top quality and fully approved, as demonstrated by Dave Metcalfe.

With more World Championship wins to his credit than any other driver, Markku Alén knows the importance of proper clothing.

INTERNATIONAL HELMET STANDARDS

CERTIFIED TO BRITISH STANDARD
1380001
BS6658-85   TYPE A

(GB)   BS 6658–85 TYPE 'A' (note Type B *not* acceptable

SNELL
MEMORIAL
FOUNDATION
ESTABLISHED 1957

(USA)

Snell SA85

Both these helmet standards are recognised by the RACMSA at time of publication.

acceptable national markings, thereby making it conform to RACMSA regulations. The number of types and makes of helmet that are now fully approved is considerable and any list would quickly be out of date, but the following list shows acceptable standard marks at the time of publication:

The R.A.C. Motor Sports Association now recognise all the above standards. Helmets are – or should be – checked by the scrutineer before most major rallies and it is important that yours carries the approval number. Stickers to indicate that they are of an approved type have to be carried on helmets and R.A.C. scrutineers will issue the latest labels showing the date of expiry of the helmet.

The RACMSA operates a security labelling system and stickers are colour

Non-helmet intercom sets are used by crews on the road sections of international events but are banned on British road rallies. Malcolm Wilson wears the Peltor model.

Crash helmets are only considered to be acceptable when the RACMSA approval sticker is affixed on the outside of the helmet.

coded. Extensive research with helmet manufacturers and International Accident Research units has revealed that the standards reached in the manufacture of a helmet do not necessarily continue indefinitely – a life of four years is now the accepted limit.

Make sure that the helmets are stored properly within the car. Do not throw helmets on the back seat after a stage as they are a confounded nuisance rolling around inside the rear of the car and, in any case, it doesn't do them much good. Make a couple of boxes or brackets to carry the helmets but remember to position these so that you can reach them easily, preferably

when wearing your seatbelts. Foam holders are available, but make sure they conform to fire regulations.

Intercoms

The engine noise inside a modern rally car is quite considerable and even worse when complemented by the sound of stones hitting the underside of the body. Therefore an intercom is desirable if the crew wish to communicate with each other clearly which, of course, they will when the co-driver is reading pace notes or route instructions to the driver. There must be no chance of an instruction being misunderstood so a good two-way intercom is essential. Not only will the driver wish to hear a co-driver's route instructions, he may also wish to give instructions during the course of the stage. Some drivers will ask their co-drivers to switch on the windscreen wipers, the auxiliary fuel pump, or flick a fuel tank switch during an event.

Having selected the intercom, make sure it is expertly fitted or is an integral part of the helmet; holes bored in a helmet weaken it and even nullify the British Standard Institute certificate. If your intercom has a boom mike make sure that this is flexible and made of a soft material, otherwise you may lose your front teeth in an accident.

Most professional crews prefer an intercom which is fitted to their full-face helmets; the Swedish 'Peltor' model of intercom being extremely reliable. It is better if the co-driver or driver can hear himself through the intercom when he speaks to his partner because the co-driver will then tend to read pace notes and give instructions at the correct volume for easy listening (it will also prevent him from blowing out his driver's ear drums and, more importantly, let him know that he can be heard by the driver even if the engine noise level is high).

One use of non-helmet headsets is during the practice or 'recce' for a rally, when it makes the job of writing and checking notes much easier. Crews also wear these headsets when driving on a road section of a stage rally or on a long, non-special stage event such as the Safari Rally.

Fitting the intercom in the car is important; it must be securely mounted. If fitted to the roll cage (the ideal place as it can be switched on and off easily) see that it can't drop off during bumpy going. Make sure that all electrical connections are good and regularly inspected and ensure that the leads from the helmet have simple jack-plug ends so that they can be pulled out easily.

Licences

One piece of 'equipment' which every crew member must carry is a competition licence. This takes the form of a club membership card for closed-to-club' rallies or an RACMSA licence for other events. Licence fees and qualification requirements

An RACMSA Log Book is necessary if you plan to enter British Special Stage events other than Internationals.

alter from time to time but, as a guide the accompanying table shows the sort of fees you can expect.

If you plan to enter British special stage events (other than Internationals) your car will need a Log Book which can be obtained from your local RACMSA scrutineer who will complete the form and send it to the MSA for verification. Once returned it has to be shown at each event. The idea of this is to maintain some continuity and ensure that scrutineers' comments from one event are seen on following ones; it is a safety precaution.

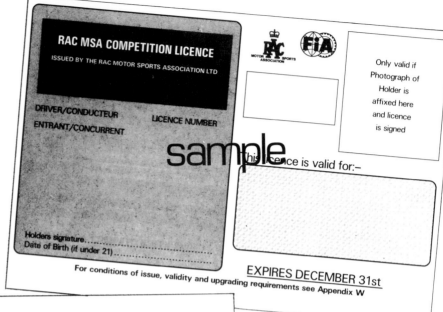

A sample of an RACMSA Competition Licence. To be valid, a licence must be signed and carry a photograph of the holder.

Licence fees for rallying		
Driver:	International	£57.00
(can also be entrant)	National	£26.00
	Restricted	£17.00
Navigator:		£17.00
(non-driver)		
Advertising permits:	International	£290.00
	National	£143.00
	Restricted	£65.00
Trade entrants	All grades	£58.00
		(all prices include VAT)

Refreshments

Food and drink are of absorbing interest to most rally drivers, consequently navigators will find it one of their chores to 'feed and water' their drivers regularly. Although the days of picnic hampers laden with chicken legs and champagne have long since passed, it is necessary to carry a few tit-bits in a rally car because sensible food and drink can refresh a crew when its energy is waning.

Sandwiches and items that deteriorate are not a good idea nor are messy, crumbly or intricately wrapped foods. Most works drivers carry a small supply of boiled sweets, Polo mints, glucose tablets, and possibly apples. Cheese can fall into the 'messy' category but a number of drivers swear by it.

Take a bottle of orange squash, lemonade, glucose drink or mineral water but keep it tightly secured within the car and avoid very 'gassy' mineral waters as they are likely to cascade all over your car when the tops are removed.

A cup of hot coffee is an excellent reviver in the middle of the night but vacuum flasks seldom survive more than one rally so you may either rely on cafés kept open for controls by organisers or leave the supply of coffee to your service crew. Although the role of the service crew is dealt with in a later chapter, it is worth mentioning that a good service crew will always provide food and drink for its drivers. Works crews may enjoy soup, coffee, sandwiches, cheese, yoghurts, biscuits or whatever specialities they desire.

Some major factory teams have various hospitality motorhomes in which their drivers can be fed. One team actually employed a Cordon Bleu cook at one time and many

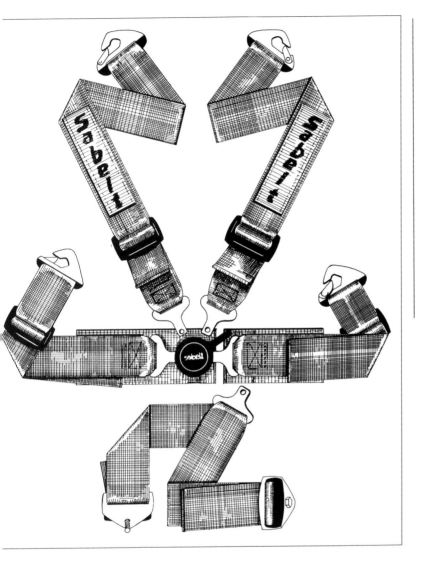

others employ specially trained people to supply food high in nutrition and energy-giving value.

Some drivers carry a set of goggles in case the windscreen pops out, some carry a knife, a crowbar, sunglasses (very important), spare socks or a spare ignition key fastened to the zip of their rally jacket. You'd be surprised how many rally crews have incurred time penalties when they couldn't unlock their car after a control because they'd lost the ignition key!

Finally, if you have a lucky charm and think it makes you drive better then by all means carry it – confidence is half the battle and you'll need all the luck you can get.

There's one more fairly important piece of equipment to consider of course – a car, so let us move on to the next chapter. ■

A good rally harness is essential. On the Sabelt 'professional' model a 'crutch strap' is offered for added security! Note the parachute-type quick release rotary buckle on this model.

GROUP THERAPY

When you first take up rallying on club events, almost any car will be eligible and you will be unlikely to face severe scrutineering. When choosing a car, don't buy anything way beyond your experience or ability – it will be costly and could be dangerous. Find out if the bug has really bitten you before you buy anything potent.

The classified columns of the enthusiast magazines offer some tempting machinery, but take care! It may be cheaper to start with an unmodified secondhand car that has had "normal" usage and add lights, necessary safety items to it, rather than buy a once glorious machine that is tired and at the end of its life.

If a car is advertised as having won its class on such-and-such a rally – so what? It's your driving ability that will count, not the previous owner's. There's quite a lot of tired old rubbish on offer so do get expert, down-to-earth advice if you are not mechanically minded. Seek advice too if it seems likely that a car you are eyeing may become ineligible for the sort of rallies you are likely to be doing. (As an extreme and, we hope, never to be repeated example, many manufacturers were left with 200 Group B cars on their hands when the category was cancelled at six months notice!).

Obviously any car you buy should

Scrutineering can be an important – if somewhat long-winded – part of a major event. At major rallies it can be something of a spectator attraction.

AUTOMOBILE CLUB D'ITALIA
COMMISSIONE SPORTIVA AUTOMOBILISTICA ITALIANA
FEDERATION INTERNATIONALE DU SPORT AUTOMOBILE

Homologation N°
Omologazione N°

A - 5 3 5 5

Groupe
Gruppo **A/B**

FICHE D'HOMOLOGATION CONFORME A L'ANNEXE J DU CODE SPORTIF INTERNATIONAL
SCHEDA D'OMOLOGAZIONE CONFORME ALL'ALLEGATO J AL CODICE SPORTIVO INTERNAZIONALE

Homologation valable à partir du
Omologazione valida a partire dal _____ **0 1 MARS 199_** _____

en groupe
in gruppo _____ **A**

Photo A
Foto A

Photo B
Foto B

1. DEFINITIONS / DEFINIZIONI

101. Contructeur
Costruttore _____ L A N C I A _____

102. Dénomination(s) commerciale(s) — Modèle et type
Denominazione(1) commerciale(1) — Modello e tipo _____ DELTA HF integrale _____

103. Cylindrée totale
Cilindrata totale _____ 1995 x 1,7 = 3391,5 _____ cm3

104. Mode de construction
Tipo di costruzione

☐ séparée, matériau du châssis
☐ separata, materiale del telaio _____
☒ monocoque
☒ monoscocca _____ acier - acciaio _____

105. Nombre de volumes
Numero dei volumi _____ 2 _____

106. Nombre de places
Numero dei posti _____ 5 _____

F.I.S.A.

1

---

comply with legal requirements but as you move up the competition tree on to more ambitious events, you will also have to pay attention to the motor sport regulations for vehicles allowed to take part in rallies.

Homologation

Before a car can compete on a major event it must be 'homologated' for sporting purposes by the manufacturer. Homologation is not as painful as it sounds; it simply means the manufacturer lists the technical specification of a car on a Form of Recognition which also incorporates lots of photographs. The Form has to be signed by a senior official of the manufacturing company – as a check on honesty – and once the Form is validated, it becomes a virtual 'birth certificate' for the car; scrutineers can check a car against its Form to see that it complies with the rules.

At the moment cars can compete in two groups, as follows:-

Group N

This is for large scale series production cars (at least 5000 built in twelve consecutive months up to 1992, 2500 thereafter) running virtually unmodified except for safety items such as competition brake material

A page from an FIA homologation form – virtually a 'birth certificate' for car and essential before it can be used in major competition.

Some rallies have fairly 'free for all' regulations which means cars do not have to be homologated. Manufacturers sometimes use such events to try out future models. Here the Escort Cosworth is on its way to a win in Spain two years before it actually goes into production.

and roll cages. It is becoming an important group and one where up and coming drivers can get attention before moving up to:

Group A

This is also for large scale production touring cars with at least 5000 built in twelve consecutive months (up to 1992, 2500 thereafter) but with greater freedom for modifications. Cars in Group A may be fettled through finishing and scraping, provided the original parts can still be identified, and engine mods allow a free camshaft profile. Chassis reinforcement is permitted and some sheet metal areas can be double-skinned. There is considerable freedom concerning suspension components, provided that the original geometry is retained and that the modified components appear in the homologation form. In general the rules are tight enough to stop you turning a rogue car into a winner, but Group A cars are not cheap and the 'homologated' specification is critical – if the car hasn't got certain things in its basic spec. (or at least listed on the form) then you can't use them! Group A cars have minimum weights and rim widths stipulated according to capacity. ∎

Make sure that your car conforms to the regulations and that you understand them – the scrutineers will. On International events the body, engine block and other major components may be marked with a special paint so that they cannot be changed.

Mud, mud, glorious mud! Kenneth Eriksson's VW Golf GTi heads for a win on the Ivory Coast Rally. For African rallies, cars must be prepared for all sorts of weather – waterproofing is essential.

The BMW M3 was specially designed for tarmac rallies – a worthwhile exercise as Bernard Beguin proved by winning the Tour de Corse. The car was privately entered by Britain's Prodrive team.

The dry, dusty tracks of Greece were ideal for Toyota's four-wheel drive Celica. This is Juha Kankkunen.

The versatile Kankkunen storms across the Sahara Desert in the frighteningly fast Group B Peugeot 205 to win the Paris-Dakar Marathon.

The Safari rally is still unique and can be very wet if the rains arrive!

Rallying has never really
caught on in North America
although the Olympus Rally
provided superb rallying
country.

The City of Coventry has boasted one of Britain's top rally teams for over three decades. It survived various name-changes – Rootes, Chrysler, Talbot then Peugeot – but it achieved great successes under the leadership of Team Boss Des O'Dell.

Rallying in Portugal always attracts big crowds. Young Alexandro Fiorio entertains this group in the Lancia Delta.

The Lombard RAC Rally is unique and still presents one of the greatest rallying challenges. Markku Ålen's Lancia tackles one of the bleakest sections.

New Zealander 'Possum' Bourne is one of the top drivers 'down under'. He's shown here on Rally Australia – a superb World Championship event.

Welcoming crowds await winner Juha Kankkunen's Peugeot on the final stage of the Paris-Dakar Rally. Note th attendant helicopter containing mechanics and tools.

Don't cry for me Argentina! World rallying's only visit to South America brings a fast, furious event. Miki Biasion is a regular winner in the Lancia Delta.

A tired man! Twice Safari winner Hannu Mikkola – one of the greatest rally drivers of all time.

On the Lombard RAC Rally of Great Britain it can be dark, wet and miserable. Conditions that Carlos Sainz adores.

Didier Auriol flies for Lancia on the dusty Acropolis Rally in Greece.

The only all-tarmac rally in the World Championship is held in Corsica where Bruno Saby is always impressive.

CAR PREPARATION

Many sports need very little in the way of equipment – you *could* win an Olympic Gold Medal in your bare feet – but to get to the top, or even be moderately successful, in rallying, you will need a well prepared car. But first – a word of caution: don't put a spanner anywhere near a rally car until you have squarely faced up to one or two questions:

● How much can you afford to spend? A lot of rally programmes fizzle out part way through because the crew forgot to work out a proper budget.
● What type of rallies are you proposing to enter? There is no point in spending money to build a car like a tank if you are going to concentrate on smooth, tarmac rallies.
● Are you really certain that you are Britain's answer to the Scandinavians? Really sure? Because if you aren't then it doesn't make sense to build a full-blooded – and very, very, expensive – works replica. Far too many people waste money preparing cars which are way ahead of their driving ability.

So, having done our best to disillusion you, let us now move on to discuss just how you can best set out to prepare your rally car.

Study the regulations. That is simple to say but from the clangers people drop it would seem to be difficult for some people to do.

Study the regulations for your type of rallying and study the homologation form for your car until you are quite sure you know exactly what you are allowed to do. In particular it is unforgivable to be caught cheating in one of the 'one-make' rally championships. Experience has shown that in those series the odd 2 or 3 bhp doesn't make a blind bit of difference so it just isn't worth sailing close to the edge of the regulations to gain them.

Remember that if your car is new then doing any motor sport in it will almost certainly clobber your warranty!

Before you start work, try to talk to one or two people running the same make of car – they should be able to alert you to any pitfalls.

Do you have any mechanical skill? If so, or if not but you can find a friend to help you, it is worth tackling your own preparation. At one time the works teams were happiest with drivers with little mechanical knowledge; not so nowadays when testing and general sorting is so important in rallying – just as it is in Formula 1. If you do your own work on your rally car you will be more capable of fixing it during an event.

What workshop space do you have? Marriages have been broken by engine rebuilds under the bed. Remember that a stripped rally car can take up a lot of space. If you have the time and money that is how you should start: by stripping your car down to the shell. Not essential of course, and you may win rallies just by bolting on a couple of extra lights, but you will be absolutely *sure* of your car if it has had a total rebuild. But only do it if you have the space, money and manpower; don't just rip

A B C

a car to pieces under the optimistic assumption that you will be able to put it all together again. If you do decide to strip the car down then this is the time to do any welding or cutting and shutting – such as putting a fireproof bulkhead behind the rear seats. While you have the car stripped down, do what you can to block off holes so that the car stays fairly free from dust and water during a rally.

Whatever your budget limitations, you must not cut corners on safety items, so now fit an interior roll cage and make it a full-house version with tubes down the windscreen pillars. Pad the cage with rubber and cover any protruding bolts.

Next, the area which loses more rallies than anything else; the electrics. Sit quietly with a large sheet of paper and plan what is going to go where on your car and sort out your wiring accordingly. Always use the correct specification of wire for a particular load and obviously vary the colours so that you can identify things.

Don't ramble wires around the car; keep things as neat and tidy as possible. Use grommets wherever necessary and avoid sharp edges. The list goes on; connections need to be grease free and tight; battery terminals should be kept clean; fuseboxes should be accessible: fit relays to the horn and extra lamps to reduce the voltage drop. In other words pay attention to detail.

You may well decide to uprate the alternator; if so, make sure you fit the correct bracket etc., because this is a vulnerable area. If you do change the alternator don't forget to have the control box and regulator checked to suit the power and the battery – over-charging can be nearly as big a headache as undercharging.

If your wife or girl friend hasn't strangled you with a jump lead by now and you have a car with impeccable wiring, start putting the suspension back so that you can get the car onto its wheels. Don't start experimenting with suspensions, fit whatever the leading drivers of your type of car use. It is too early in your career to get neurotic over settings.

Make very sure that the bump stops work before the shock absorbers are fully compressed, otherwise you will damage the brackets or, worse, the turrets.

Spring rates and ride heights will be controlled to some extent by the type of rallies you are doing; as a general rule attempts to jack-up cars into the sky cause all sorts of other problems and aren't successful. Anyway you will be protecting your engine with one of the most important fittings: a sump guard. Get a good one and fit it properly. If you fit an expensive lightweight sump guard add a sheet of thin mild steel to it – it will be cheaper to replace this now and again if appropriate than to buy a new guard.

Use heavy duty bushes where available and fit a high ratio steering rack; don't underestimate the arm effort needed for modern high speed rallying.

Install the most appropriate final drive you can afford. Drivers always want low ratios, team managers like to play safe with high. The drivers are usually proved right!

We nearly forgot: fit a limited slip diff of course if appropriate but only if it is allowed under the regulations. It is a very easy thing for a scrutineer to check!

The interior of a modern rally car should be neat and functional. Note the driver's foot rest, brake balance bar and master cut-out switch. Otherwise most of the standard instruments and switches are retained.

Fit some form of crash hat carrier – like the one shown here which is made of foam rubber.

Mount the seats firmly and fit full safety harnesses. ▶

If the cost of all this is starting to frighten you, bear in mind that if you are an undiscovered genius then you may be able to shine in your aunt's old shopping car, but it is unlikely. You just have to accept that motor sport of any sort is going to cost you money!

So let us spend some more of your money and consider the clutch. Most standard clutches have a certain safety margin – say 10% or so – so if you are leaving your engine standard your clutch should cope. It could be better though to fit a competition one. Considering how much more reliable they make rally cars, competition clutches are quite cheap and are usually interchangeable with the standard ones.

Having taken some trouble with your axle (such as by having the best available halfshafts) and having fitted a competition clutch, now get your propshaft properly balanced before fitting it.

Remember what we said about not

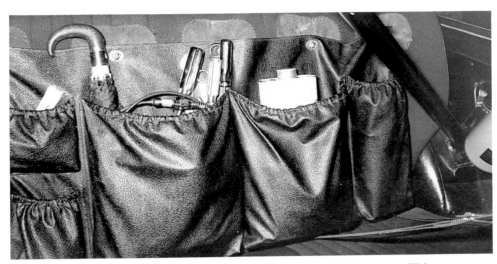

A pouch on the back seat makes a good home for tools and spares. This road-rally crew carry an umbrella in case of a wet walk home . . . Oh! Ye of little faith!

The engine compartment must be given maximum attention and everything must be as neat as possible.

Be neat in the boot too. Make sure the spare wheel is secure.

The engine compartment of a clubman's car will be a lot simpler and more straightforward but will still need to be neat and tidy and meticulously prepared.

Axles are vulnerable – note the bracing bar and skid plate fitted to this one.

Having spent money on the engine, protect it with a good sump guard.

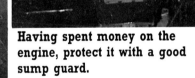

Skids on the silencer will help to protect it from damage.

economising on safety? Well, here we go again because the next item to consider is the brakes. Brake pipes must be well protected and run inside the car where possible. The flexible hoses should have protective springs coiled round them. Washers and seals should be replaced regularly – an advantage of doing you own maintenance and preparation is that you will get a feel for when this should be. Discs and drums must be running true, wheel bearings must be checked regularly, drums should be cleaned out regularly and you need competition brake fluid. All obvious things, but all important.

If you have a dual-line braking system with one cylinder operating the front brakes and another the rear you will, if the cylinders have an adjustable swinging beam between them, be able to 'tune' the balance of the braking between front and rear. But, ladies and gentlemen, this is for experts – don't waste time or money on such sophistication until you are very, very, sure that you are capable of making use of it.

With only mild power increases you should be able to stop OK if you simply fit competition brake material. Bed the pads and/or shoes in as advised by the manufacturer and if you expect to have to change during an event, bed a spare set in beforehand. If a material change isn't enough to give you proper stopping power then consult an expert before you venture into a complete system change – we don't want to lose you (we need someone to buy our next book!).

Modify the handbrake to give it a fly-off action.

Wheels? Well, a lot of people get carried away by cosmetics and fit wheels which may be prettier but are in fact heavier than standard, which is silly. Simple advice: follow the example of people who are winning in your car. Don't go overboard on rim widths.

Happily, some of the one-make rally championships are stipulating one type of tyre. Sensible, because tyre permutations and costs have done more damage to rallying than perhaps we realise. When you hear works teams talk of 1200 tyres for a car on a Monte, perhaps it is time for a still,

Spotlights flapping about do not give the driver confidence. Note the adjustable support bars and the sturdy brackets.

A boot mounted dry sump oil tank and twin fuel pumps. Neatness is vital
otherwise it can quickly become a plumber's nightmare.

And an equally neat boot mounted battery case.

This fire extinguisher on a works car is filled with low toxicity fire fighting gas and 'plumbed-in' to both cockpit and engine compartments. It is triggered by switches inside and outside the car.

small voice to cry "enough"?

Because of the competition between manufacturers – which can only benefit the clubman – it would be dangerous in this book to give advice on particular tyres because things change so quickly. Our only advice is not to burden yourself with the cost of umpteen tyre permutations until your driving deserves them. Once again – ask the leading competitors for advice but this time probe them on the puncture record of particular tyres – in your early stages you want to have trouble-free rallies while you shake yourself down; you won't get them if you are constantly changing wheels because of punctures.

Anyway, now you should have a well prepared shell fitted with a sump guard and safety cage and with a well sorted axle, prop-shaft, gearbox, etc., (we will come to the engine later). Presumably at some stage you will have had the car painted. Although rallying has improved its image over the years with the growth of sponsorship, there are still very few cars properly presented

with eye catching colour schemes. Give it a thought and if you or a mate have got styling flair you may attract attention simply because you have a well presented car. Remember too that the cleaner and crisper your car looks, the better ride you may have with scrutineers.

Now let us move inside the car. Seats are a matter for personal preference. They should be strong and firmly bolted down with zero play. The fore and aft position should be tailored for the number one driver.

Back to safety, fit the best seat belts you can get and fit them properly. You will get bounced about a lot on special stages so you must be able to strap yourself in firmly. The co-driver will probably want to sit well back in the car (out of your way as you do your 'hero driver' bit) in which case a bracing bar for his feet will be necessary so that he can push himself into his seat as he sits there counting his beads.

When did you last have an instrument fail in a standard car? Probably never. Which is a good argument for not loading your rally car with a battery of extra dials. You should have an oil gauge or warning light of course; adjust it so that you get a warning *before* any serious damage is done.

The co-driver will need a plug for his light which brings us into the realm of ergonomics (the word adds a touch of culture to the book if nothing else). Get with your co-driver and sit in the car and then decide where you are going to place his plug, any auxiliary switches, a torch holder, crash hat supports and so on. Don't mount extra switches in groups of more than three – there is a limit to how far most drivers can count.

Additional lights sometimes fall into the area of machismo. Fit what you are allowed; fit the best; mount them so that they won't wobble about; wire them properly – then forget them. Don't blame the lights if you get murdered on every night stage, find out first if you are one of those people who

simply hasn't got very good night vision. Make sure additional lights comply with the law.

Incidentally, if you are serious about saving weight (and you should be) you could perhaps have quick release plugs for auxiliary lights so that they can be removed on daylight sections (provided the regulations allow this) and carried in a support car. Only do this if it can be organised without any hassle.

Back to our ergonomics, neatness must be the watchword. Stow everything safely and carry this theory back to the boot too. Don't allow a heavy spare wheel to fly about, nor a battery for that matter which can be even more dangerous. If your boot needs a key to open it, wire one in place during a rally to save time. A safety petrol tank is nice to have, though costly of course. Locking petrol caps should be replaced before a rally – they waste time. Add bonnet clips to stop it flying up or

Fire extinguishers must be of the correct type and mounted properly.

Water, water everywhere!
Make sure your car is well
waterproofed as you're certain to
encounter wet going somewhere,
be it on a flooded Welsh lane ...

... the Lombard RAC ...

. . or a muddy quarry.

working loose – the same for the boot.

You must naturally have a fire extinguisher on board and the car must have a clearly marked external switch for the electrical circuit so that a spectator can operate it if, for instance, you are trapped in a car after a shunt.

You will need a tow rope. Oh yes you will! If you leave the back seat out you can replace it with a canvas or plastic sheet with stowage pockets and carry a tow rope in there – along with spare wiper blades, tyre levers and (for events a fair way from home) a spare gasket set.

With all the weight you have added there is something to be said for leaving the carpets at home. The car will be noisier but it will be as noisy as hell anyway with stones being hurled about underneath on forest stages. Having saved that weight, put a bit back by carrying a first aid kit.

Nearly finished the preparation saga now, but there is still one thing to consider – the engine. Eric Carlsson made a bigger impact on rallying in his day than anyone and he weighed 18 stone and his Saab had a tiny engine. In the old Mexico championship, whenever Ford's Peter Ashcroft put a few cars on a rolling road he often found the winners were a few bhp down on the rest. If it is dark, cold and wet and you are going downhill on a loose surface then power to weight is less important than driving ability, far less; which is a long winded way of saying don't waste money on engine tuning until your driving is up to it.

A basic but worthwhile improvement can be gained by simply stripping the engine and having it rebuilt under what is picturesquely called blueprinting, in other words getting everything to the best tolerance for performance. Combustion chambers can be balanced and equalised; manifolds and ports can be matched precisely and so on. Probably more trouble

The early pictures in this book featured no sponsors' advertising. All that has changed. Lamp covers are a 'high exposure' area and if the spotlights are removed in daytime or, if the lights are in use at night, the make of light is never in doubt as a spotlamp cover is mounted directly onto the bodywork. What will they think of next?

And speaking of spotlights, there's quite a variety to choose from.

Prime advertising sites are the bonnet . . . ▲

. . and even the bumper. ▶

If your car is sponsored make sure that signwriting is top quality. And take care to apply stickers neatly.

than it is worth for average rallying – more relevant to production car racing perhaps, but if you do it you may feel the car is quicker and have more confidence as a result (and confidence is half the battle) and at least the stripping and rebuilding will give you an intimate knowledge of your engine.

If you get involved in more elaborate engine tuning we recommend that you aim for mid-range torque rather than out-and-out top-end performance. It may be impressive at the bar to mention casually a high bhp figure but if it is only achieved at very high revs (and your gearing means that you only reach it after seven miles flat-out on Pendine Sands) it won't exactly do you much good on rallies. But then not too many rallies are won at the bar nowadays, otherwise the results tables would be vastly different.

The key phrase under more general tuning is 'machining and polishing' because if the regulations permit you can clearly improve engine performance by raising compression and generally improving the

gas flow. But – and we hate to keep preaching but we are trying to save you money – go for reliability and when possible copy the experts (and in your case an 'expert' should be regarded as someone who finishes fairly well up regularly i.e., with a reliable car).

Rallying has its opponents and noise is quoted as one of the sport's most irritating features, so fit a good exhaust system and make sure it will stay in place. You have decided to take up rallying so that you can have a roarty car to impress the birds? Well, we admire your rather muddled motives but could you possibly clear-off and take up another sport?

Even a standard exhaust system will have a longer life if you strengthen it with a support bracket attached to the bellhousing: you should also tack weld all the joints in the system to keep it in one piece. Add 'skids' of mild steel strip to each end of the silencer box – as well as at any other vulnerable points – to stop the box being knocked off on rocks. Sooner or later you will have to reverse in a fairly narrow

Switches for battery mains and fire extinguisher must be readily accessible outside the car in case the crew are trapped in an accident.

Regulations require crew names to be lettered on the outside of the car on international events. On club rallies it is not a requirement and may be as well when there are frequent co-driver changes!

space; if your exhaust pipe sticks out at the back it will get filled with earth. Keep it short.

In theory the car should now be nearly ready for its first event. But pause. Go over the car carefully.

Any bolts sticking out where they can catch against a pipe or wire? Any bolts sticking out which could catch against you if you roll over? Any brackets which you bodged-up in a hurry and which spoil the overall look of the car? Remake them.

Jack, tools, wheelbrace, first aid kit, sweeties all carefully stowed? Sponsor's stickers neatly displayed?

Can you get full throttle?

When you are satisfied on all these things take your baby out, grit your teeth and drive it in anger over a local rough road. Go on, force yourself. If it won't survive a couple of miles of this, how do you expect it to survive a rally?

Often things which are going to come loose will do so in the first couple of miles –

better that these are test miles, rather than an actual event. When you get back from the test run, check everything again, then wash and polish the car before you report to the start of a rally.

Service

Some events allow service. Many argue against it – including at times the works teams who are horrified at the cost of planes and such like.

If you are on a rally and works teams are present don't expect the works mechanics to mother you in your privately owned car. They will have different priorities. In fact the only real way to grab their attention is to go so well that you end up beating the works cars. But it ain't easy.

If you put out your own service car please do not set it high average speeds between service points. Too many mechanics have had accidents that way, and do tell the crew not to leave litter behind them.■

A comparatively new name in rallying – the Daihatsu Charade on the Scottish Rally.

RALLY DRIVING

Have you had a medical check recently? Are your eyes OK? If you wear glasses have you had them tested lately?

All points worth considering before you try to become a rally driver. Not much point in spending a lot of money on extra lights if your eyes need testing. Not much point in shaving a few grams off the weight of your car if you've got a bulbous belly.

Don't get us wrong – you don't have to be a superman to do well on rallies and certainly you don't have to be as fit as say, a marathon runner or sprinter. But consider for a moment . . . the standard of competition is high so doesn't it make sense to get yourself in the best possible shape before you start rallying?

If nothing else, if you are fit you will be better able to push your car out of a stage if you have a breakdown.

One other thing before you start rally driving. Have you been to one of the rally schools? Worth doing because although you may have to lay out £100 or so, it is better to do this than to spend a lot more on preparing a car only to find that you have little or no basic aptitude. If you make this unhappy discovery at a rally school but decide to plough on, at least the knowledge can steer you in the right direction regarding cars and preparation.

One rather important benefit of a rally school is that it should give you a chance to sit with a star driver and study his technique.

Having decided to continue, you now need to get yourself into gear – overalls, crash hat, gloves, shoes and so on. No need to go berserk on your equipment at the beginning but let us repeat what we said in an earlier chapter: make sure clothing is practical and comfortable. Don't wear anything new for the first time on an event;

if your new fireproof underpants choke you (you may have your own priorities on what you want to protect) find out before, not on, a rally. We made the point in car preparation that the sport needs smart presentation so please don't turn up at the start of a rally in greasy, torn overalls. Keep an old pair for working on the car, a better pair for driving in.

Medical experts reckon that it takes up to thirty minutes for your eyes to adjust to darkness after being in bright lights . . . so carry sunglasses to put on at night controls, where there may be TV lights and photographers' flash guns. Obviously you will also need the sunglasses on bright days. Night driving glasses are not recommended.

Once you have fitted yourself out with proper clothing and equipment, you need to blend yourself with your car. Can you reach all the controls when you are strapped in? Are you happy with the pedals? Is the seat mounted properly for you? Most drivers seem happier with more of a sit-up-and-beg driving position than that adopted by racing drivers – it obviously helps to be able to see enough to 'place' a car. Don't have the seat ludicrously high of course, otherwise you will end up as the Hunchback of Knotty Ash!

If you like a wheel with a turquoise sheepskin cover then fit one duckie, but don't expect it to make you any quicker. There is really not much wrong with standard steering wheels but if you feel happier with something different then please – be our guest.

Remember that a steering wheel is not intended as an additional grab handle, just for steering.

Don't bother too much with fine tuning the suspension and brakes until you have a

Rallying's superstars . . .

Juha Kankkunen (Finland)

'Miki' Biasion (Italy)

Carlos Sainz (Spain)

Didier Auriol (France)

Kenneth Eriksson (Sweden)

Timo Salonen (Finland)

The best of British . . .

David Llewellin

Malcolm Wilson

Gwyndaf Evans

Dave Metcalfe

Colin McRae

Louise Aitken-Walker

little experience, nor should you become obsessive about tyre pressures.

You may have your own views on how you want to set your lights – clearly they mustn't irritate non-competing cars coming the other way – but do remember to set the lights with the car fully laden in rally trim. That means with your co-driver onboard.

This poor devil is the guy who can rarely win a rally for you, but he can certainly lose one, so choose him/her with care. In fact in your early days it is worth doing a rally or two as a navigator yourself, this will give you some idea of the problems the co-driver faces and therefore the qualities you need to look for in one. Several top drivers started as navigators. If you are totally without experience then you are not going to get the star co-drivers leaping into your car so you will just have to look for someone who is pleasant to get on with and, hopefully, a disciplined thinker and good at figures. Note that "pleasant to get on with"

is listed first. Let's face it: rallying is a sport which should be done for fun – why put up with a miserable sod just because he is a good co-driver?

Can your proposed co-driver drive? Will you be able to rest while he steers you from one special stage to another? Has he driving ambitions of his own? (if so turn through 180 degrees and run away as fast as you can).

Can he/does he write for any of the motoring papers? If so it may help you to get assistance from overseas rallies which may be glad of media coverage.

Practice

Now you have sorted out yourself and your car and found a co-driver, don't set off for a rally just yet. Practise first.

Go out over local roads (at night) and shake yourself down as a crew. Get used to each other's language (it may get colourful under stress). Practise wheel changing; few

The pedals must be adjusted until the driver is completely happy with them. Note the support for the left foot – don't use the clutch as a resting place!

crews do but it can save vital seconds on a stage if you know where everything is stowed and who is going to do what during the wheel change. Practise wearing full rally gear including crash hats!

Watch some of the top works pairings in action – or for that matter, the more professional non-works crews – and you'll begin to appreciate what the sport is about.

By this stage you should have enough confidence to concentrate on how to become a better driver, safe in the knowledge that you have taken care as far as possible of all the factors contributing to success – the car, co-driver, etc.

If you want to become a star driver (or simply a competent clubman) then it sounds obvious but as we said earlier there is one thing you must do above all else and that is drive. Drive everything and anything at every opportunity. Hannu Mikkola had a season of saloon car racing based on Rochdale (very character forming) and it put an edge on his driving. We are not suggesting you need a full season of club

racing but certainly a few races will give you a wider appreciation of speed. Autotests, rallycross, autocross – anything; if it has four wheels and an engine, then drive it.

Keep records. In other words log all the events you do, making a note of other competitors and how you fared against them (so that you can see if you are improving if you meet them later). Log where you finished, how many starters, how well the event was run, any marshall-ing problems, any difficulty in getting hotels, any problems in finding the start, and so on and so on. The sort of thing which will help you to do better on the event the following year.

There is something to be said for a season or so of road events before you tackle the tougher stage rallies – it will certainly bed you in as a crew. When you do get onto stage events you will quickly realise the obvious: rallies are won or lost on corners. Given the right sized wellie anyone can drive fast in a straight line. You

A cross section of Pirelli's rally tyres.

Left to right:
1. MS 90 A forest tyre for use when the surface is loose and wet. Notice the open pattern. Generally speaking the more open the pattern the better it is for loose going.
2. SG 90 Similar to MS 90 but for use when the surface is slightly harder.
3. S 990 A wider version.
4. SG 35 For use on loose or rocky dry roads.
5. 'Monte Carlo' For use on asphalt stages where conditions are damp or where there is dust or dirt. Notice the tread pattern – this is cut by hand.
6. 'Rain' For use on asphalt stages where water is standing.
7. 'Slick' For use on totally dry asphalt.

There are various rubber compounds which drivers may specify for tyres – these improve the grip even more, depending on conditions.

Part of a major team's tyre stock prior to a major event. Note the crayon markings to indicate grooves which will be hand cut.

71

Spectators can be off-putting to a driver – even on the Safari.

must learn to corner well.

The technique is obviously governed by the type of car you are in and the road surface. If you are on dry tarmac then the neatness of a racing driver is appropriate. Incidentally, note how most of the sideways Formula One men eventually settle down to a more controlled line. A smooth line is particularly important with the lower-powered one-make championships – hurl the car about too much and you will scrub off all your speed. But even if the road is dry and the sun is shining and the birds are singing you must cultivate one thing; determination.

You must want to win. You must want to will the blasted car to the end of the stage. You must shut your mind to anything but that one objective, getting the car to the finish as fast as possible.

Experience at the Ford Rally School indicated that people just will not concentrate. It's not easy to maintain concentration and determination when it's cold, wet and windy and you've just had a puncture but maintaining concentration is the key to success.

On the loose

If you concentrated when on tarmac, you will have to concentrate just as hard on loose surfaces. If you are enough of an enthusiast to have bought this book and waded this far you will probably have seen one of the excellent rally films and videos there are about. If so you will have noticed one thing: cars – at least rear wheel drive ones – don't always go round corners in a conventional fashion. The back ends of the cars are swinging this way and that.

This is because if you drive round a loose corner in the conventional way in a rear wheel drive car, as you speed up you will understeer off the road. Note when the first ice of winter hits the country how many people slide off into ditches on the outside of bends; in other words they have understeered off. The same thing will happen on a loose special stage unless you set up the car to stop it. Purists may argue that you could tune suspensions to remove the understeer but they forget that the surfaces are loose and sometimes rough, which tends to clobber the theory.

If you are approaching a left-hand bend on a loose surface and deliberately put the car into an unstable situation by a sharp turn on the steering wheel to the right, you will then be able to flick or 'pendulum' the car back round to the left to go round the corner and because of the controlled (at least we hope it is controlled) instability you will avoid going off through understeer. It may look like one long accident looking for somewhere to happen when you see it for the first time, but it can be safer and faster. Obviously humps and bumps may throw you off your intended line in the middle of a corner so you must be ready to correct immediately. Don't overdo the see-sawing about of course if it results in scrubbing off too much speed. It is all a question of balance, control and experience; for four wheel drive cars a smoother approach in more of a racing line will be better.

The ability to have a car under control on a loose surface is the key to success on special stages. At the rally schools you will find yourself asked to drive round and round a single pylon – holding the car on line with throttle control. This not only teaches car control – it makes people realise that you have to work hard and concentrate.

If all else fails and a slide off the road seems inevitable you still have one friend left: the handbrake. If you are doing 25 mph or so, then yank on the steering wheel and at the same time de-clutch and tug at the handbrake (which should be the fly-off type) you will find, to your co-driver's surprise (and possibly yours) that you have turned through 180 degrees; it can be done in roads only slightly wider than the car is long. Both authors during misspent youths as navigators have overshot turnings and been pivoted through 180 degrees by drivers doing handbrake turns.

Don't practise it on public roads. Find somewhere quiet and loose and keep doing it until you can judge the right amount of effort and sharpness to put into your actions. Once you have mastered it you can use the technique to spin to a stop if you are in danger of going off and, with practise, you will be able to use the handbake to induce the instability we talked about and hence help your general cornering particularly on hairpins. Caution though – don't get neurotic about it, concentrate on your general driving technique first.

The same applies to the dreaded left-foot braking which mainly applies to front-wheel-drive cars. It is a much discussed technique and can work well but you must practise and practise again to make a success of it.

The big problem with front-wheel-drive cars when driven in anger is that as you apply the power the front wheels may lose their grip, which in turn induces understeer, which can be terminal if you don't do something about it. The Scandinavians worked out that if you keep your right foot on the accelerator and put your left foot on the brake you can control the rear wheels through the braking system, while your right foot (and hopefully the steering too of course) controls the front end. Using the left foot on the brakes makes the back end come round, just as the handbrake does. For the same reason most drivers have their brakes biased towards the rear.

The brakes being on while the accelerator is pressed can also act as something of a limited slip, although if you are too enthusiastic with the left foot you will simply slow yourself down.

Bear in mind that unless you are very careful you will burn out your brakes and be no quicker, so let us repeat: only try it when you have explored and mastered the other techniques. Try to see the old Castrol film of the Flying Finns which features Timo Makinen vividly demonstrating the technique in a Mini. He makes it quite clear that you have to change gear without using the clutch, which may be less than appealing if you are buying your own gearboxes!

In theory you can use the same left foot technique on front engined, rear-wheel-drive cars but it must be stressed that more rallies are won without using it. The idea is that it helps you to balance a car better and that in particular it can help you take off properly before a brow so that you 'fly' at the right angle. Stig Blomqvist certainly advocates this.

Incidentally if a brow is 'blind' try not to approach it in a straight line. The Scandinavians work on the reasonable theory that if someone has taken the trouble to build a road through a forest and up a hill, then presumably they have continued the road on the other side of the hill but (and there so often is a 'but' in rallying) there may be a T-junction just the other side. If you fly majestically over the brow pointing straight ahead, you may well exit from the rally through the fence which is also straight ahead.

If you come over with the car slightly out

Rally drivers must be versatile. Different techniques are required for mud . . .

Gravel . . .

On tarmac . . .

of line (in the unstable position we talked about earlier) then you will be better placed to flick the car round the corner.

We are all clear that all this is taking place on roads closed to other traffic aren't we . . .? Good.

Snow and ice

If you wake up one morning and the roads are covered in snow, don't go back to bed. Get out and practise.

We see snow so rarely in Britain that it makes sense to use every opportunity to get the feel of driving on it. You will need to use similar techniques to driving on the loose and the same applies to sheet ice of course. Note by the way that under slippery conditions, top drivers will de-clutch if all is lost. Removing the drive from the wheels makes things as smooth as possible and may keep you in control of the situation. Practise this if possible.

On a rally in snow your running order is critical, as is the track of your car. If you have a different track from everyone else you may find yourself having to plough through virgin snow all the time.

For known snowy conditions you may on some events be allowed to use studded tyres. Our advice? Ask the tyre companies if they have any good secondhand studded tyres left over from previous years and use those. The top drivers will sometimes get into a sweat over this make of stud or that type of bonding – just as skiers argue over the best type of preparation for their skis – but when the chips or flakes are down it all hinges on how quick the driver is.

What else? Oh yes. Fog! Horrid stuff but you will meet it sooner or later. No known technique for seeing through it. If someone passes you, try to hang on to them, at the risk of following the District Nurse into her drive.

In Formula One it seems to be an accepted tactic to make it difficult for another driver to get past. Not so in rallying. If someone catches you up it

And on 'odd-ball' events like America's Pikes Peak hill climb, a flat-out blind up a mountain.

**Club drivers can succeed
... Paul Frankland**

Mark Higgins

means they are quicker than you are, so get out of the way as soon as you can. Never baulk other cars.

It is a few pages since we last mentioned it so let us remind you again: concentrate. Concentrate in fog. Concentrate in rain and don't forget to concentrate on easy road sections. If you are chatting about your heroic performance on the last stage some of the shine will be taken off if you hit the back of a milk-float through not paying attention.

In the split of duties the driver should really be the one in touch with the mechanical needs of the car so as you are running into a fuel stop, control or overnight halt, dictate a list of 'jobs to be done' to the co-driver, and try to put things in order of priority. The fact that your jelly-baby holder has come loose is slightly less important than that the exhaust is falling off. If, sadly, you are faced with a major job – such as a gearbox change – the co-driver should be working out exactly how much time will be in hand both before and after the stop, while you think through how to tackle the job.

With experience you should be able to pace yourself. We say "should" although this does seem to take some young drivers a long time.

Learn when to pull out all the stops and above all learn never to give up. If you make a porridge of a stage, keep going – the stage may be cancelled for some reason.

Never give up unless of course you have a major accident. You need also to recognise that if you are trying hard and hoping to go places, then sooner or later you are going to have an accident. Rallying is a relatively safe sport but there are no special techniques for having happy accidents, although it does seem as if some drivers bear charmed lives – or have such developed reflexes that they can stay in touch with things later than lesser mortals.

Don't misunderstand us – we are not advocating an irresponsible approach which puts you in a ditch on every rally. What we are saying is that if you are to find your limit then sooner or later you are likely to overcook things and come unstuck. How you learn from the experience and how you progress as a result will dictate just how good a driver you become.

Two final points on rally driving: *never* try to improve your performance by taking drugs. They are unlikely to make you quicker, they could mar your judgement and cause an accident. Most important of all, rallying just doesn't need the drug taking scandals which beset other sports.

Finally, avoid driving with windows open – a major cause of injury in crashes according to rally medical officers; the temptation (foolishly) to put your arm out to stop a car turning over is very strong – and very dangerous! ■

RALLY NAVIGATION

Having devoted a chapter to developing the prima ballerinas it is now time to introduce the corps de ballet, that brave body always destined to play the role of bridesmaids, the poor little Cinderellas hidden away from the limelight – the navigators or co-drivers!

The navigator/co-driver enjoys little of the glamour but most of the worries, (ever counted the number of co-drivers with grey hair/no hair/ulcers?) At the professional level the co-driver only earns a fraction of the top drivers' fees yet frequently finds himself the subject of abuse and criticism and ends up with all the dirty jobs.

In the event of a breakdown it will be the co-driver who walks for miles over frozen moorland to summon help whilst the driver sleeps in a cosy rug. Before the rally it will be the co-driver who sits in his hotel room checking his pace-notes and studying the regulations while the driver goes to a glittering pre-rally reception. After being thrown about and pummelled on the rally it will be the co-driver who misses the post-rally dinner because he is checking the results. Blessed are the meek.

The sole redeeming feature of navigating is that it is the cheapest way into the sport, and if you're lucky enough to reach the very top and sit alongside the world's greatest drivers as part of a Works Team you'll appreciate the privileged position you occupy; all the horrors and hardships will have been worth it.

However, before we discuss the craft at which you'll need to become perfect, let us briefly discuss the terminology used in describing the poor creature, for he doesn't even possess a proper title!

Basically the navigator tends to be so-called when he's conducting the map work on a road event and where he will never be expected to touch the steering wheel. Co-drivers were originally called such on the bigger Internationals where navigation was not too difficult and where they might be required to drive, albeit on easier sections.

Now the term co-driver is used for the passenger on even the smallest stage event when there is absolutely no likelihood of his taking the wheel. On anything but a navigational road rally we should really describe him as the Office Manager for that is what he is – a highly organised office manager who can drive safely (if he has to give his precious partner a rest) and who probably has a good knowledge of psychology, mathematics, languages, geography and economics. If you qualify on all counts, telephone your nearest team manager immediately. If you fail to qualify, don't worry, we've yet to find anyone who does.

A good navigator (and we'll call him that for the rest of this chapter) will start by gaining as much experience as possible in every type of event from the smallest treasure hunt upwards. He will be a keen motor club member – probably be involved in running events and committee work as all this develops the ability to organise, which is the navigator's job. By helping to organise rallies one begins to understand the workings of organisers' minds and this

The driver can help his navigator by reading out route instructions and map references, providing these are supplied before the start.

Navigators should always make it as easy as possible for marshals. Holding a light above the time card will help. And make sure the time card is clipped to a board.

can be very useful for a competitor.

The navigator will be a tidy-minded individual and will keep everything in its place in the car, and although he will let the driver look after the mechanical bits he will know where the jack, the spare fuses and the tow-rope are stowed.

Equipment

The most important, and probably the first item to be purchased by a navigator will be a map. Assuming you are starting in British rallies this will inevitably come from the glorious range of Ordnance Survey maps, most likely one of the 1:50,000 series; these give a scale of approximately $1^1/4$ inches to the mile and are used by all British rally organisers. The organisers of any rally will specify the maps to be used on the event, and you should obtain these maps in good time and prepare them for the rally.

Ordinance Survey maps are easily obtainable and there is an official stocklist in practically every town. It is advisable to purchase your maps from one stockist so that you build up a relationship with the retailer; they may then be more helpful

when you require maps quickly which are out of stock.

When you buy your Ordnance Survey Map you will notice that it is covered by thin lines forming small squares – these lines are part of the National Grid which covers the country and is based on a point in the English Channel, south-west of Land's End. The figures by the lines along the edges of the map represent their distances in kilometres, east and north of this origin. If total measurements from the point off Lands End were taken, the number of kilometres would be too large for practical use, so the figures are repeated every 100 kilometres and each 100 kilometre square is designated by two letters. The small diagram on the bottom of each map shows the incidence of grid letters on it. You will rarely, if ever, encounter the letters on a rally, the actual map being indicated by its number and you'll become very familiar with these map numbers and know that sheet 136 is "Newtown and Llandloes", sheet 95 is the Isle of Man and so on.

When plotting a map reference always plot 'eastings' first; these are the numbers printed along the top and bottom edges of the map. Next plot the 'northings' – the

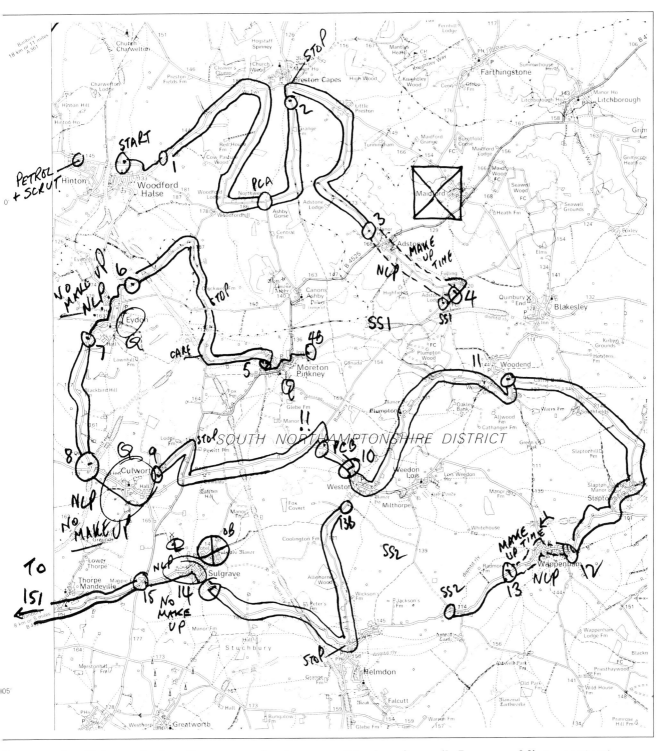

The route should be marked on the map as clearly as possible, in soft pencil. Arrows and lines must not obscure any bends or roads to be used. Note how clearly 'Out of Bounds' areas are marked, as are 'Quiet Areas', 'Stop' junctions and 'No Lateness Penalty' sections. Note that extra comments have been taken from the roadbook and added by the navigator e.g. "Care", "Make up time" and direction of approach after a triangle which might easily be missed. Special Stage starts and finishes are marked clearly but no markings are shown on the stage in accordance with RACMSA regulations. This route is given purely as an example of how you might like to mark your map – it is not an actual rally.

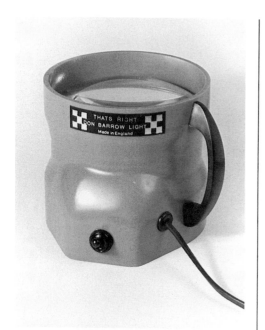

An illuminated map magnifier is necessary for road rally navigators and also used by stage co-drivers if the route of stages is read from a map. This one is made in strong PVC and carries a powerful lens and bulb. For British use a Romer baseplate is incorporated.

numbers printed down both sides. There are several catch phrases to help you to remember which to plot first, one of the more printable being "along the passage and up the stairs". In other words, first look along the bottom edge, then up the sides. To make it easier to plot a reference, every tenth grid line is printed slightly heavier than the rest. In a six figure reference the first three figures represent tens, units and tenths of kilometres east and the last three represent those to the north. With practise you should become adept at plotting references and the more expert navigators can manage at least two or three a minute when stationary and can also keep up a healthy batting average when the car is moving.

Practise plotting as much as you can and you'll soon speed up – but always take extra care with references like 010101 or 696969. In order to give you a really accurate plot (possibly a road beside a grass triangle – beloved by rally organisers) you may be given an eight figure reference, but it is more common for organisers to stick to 'halves' and so a reference will be shown as 100½200½ (or, as some purists may prefer, 10052005).

On the latest Ordnance Survey maps (second series 1:50,000) the 'eastings' and 'northings' are marked at intervals across the maps which makes for quicker plotting. You may wish to add a few more of your own as well.

In order to plot references quickly and accurately it is necessary to use a "romer". This is a small plastic device, of which there are several makes and which is the navigator's prime tool of his trade. A romer has the scale of the map broken down into tenths and by sliding this along the maps having found the appropriate kilometre square, you can measure off the exact reference accurately and quickly. Romers can carry scales of several maps – possibly 1:50,000, 1,63,360 (the old 1 inch to the mile maps, now replaced in Britain by the 1:50,000 scale) and even 1:126720 scale; this ½ inch to the mile scale is used mostly in Ireland. The scale of 1:50,000 is, of course by far the most popular, although 1:25,000 are gaining more usage on Special Stage events.

If you are planning to use the romer only with 1:50,000 maps you might round off the other three corners so that you can find the necessary scale instantly, this can save time. The romer should be placed on a loop of string, worn round the neck – there's nothing so elusive as a 'stringless' romer in a bouncing rally car.

A road which is shown in white on the map may be passable or it may be unsurfaced and peter out into a bog or chassis-breaking impasse. In rally parlance these roads are 'goers' or 'non-goers' and as time progresses the rally navigator will gain more information about these; this information should be added to the map by 'highlighting' the roads which 'go'.

The General Regulations of the RACMSA severely restrict the amount of information you can add to your map. For road rallies only 1:50,000 maps may be used and the extra information limited to 'highlighting'

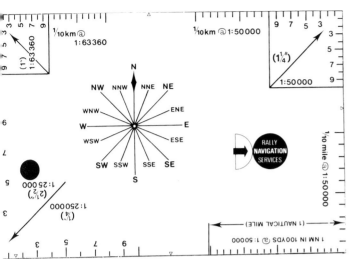

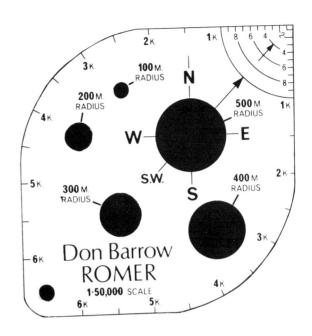

The Romer is the most important tool of the navigator's trade. There are several types. The Don Barrow model carries holes of different diameter for marking noise areas. 'Rally Navigation Services' model can be used with maps of different scales.

The British made Terratrip Rally Computers are widely used throughout the world and make life a lot easier for navigators. The '202' model has two distance displays – one for total distance and the other for interval distance. It can be calibrated for miles or kilometres and the total display can be manually adjusted – very useful after a 'wrong slot'. There is display lighting for night use and an internal rechargeable battery to keep the unit functioning if the car battery is temporarily disconnected. The '404' is the most comprehensive Terratrip model. The two right-hand displays show total distance (top) and interval distance. The left-hand displays show time of day and stopwatch but they can also be made to show speed and average speed. Among the many 'extra' functions are audible alarms which can be set for time or distance. This model also has a night light and internal re-chargeable battery.

existing information; like numbers, words and all legends printed on the map but no roads or junctions. Existing information can be repeated if necessary, such as grid numbers, map overlap marking and, of course, any information provided by the organisers of the event in which you are competing can be added in pencil but must be removed after the event.

The idea of such rules is to prevent road navigators treating the maps as pace notes and thus encourage high speeds on the road. The rules do change from time to time but the current RACMSA Year Book (the *Blue Book*) will give you the latest regulations in detail.

Maps can quickly wear at the folds, so a piece of Sellotape stuck on the backs of the corner folds can help to preserve the maps and avoid your trying to navigate your driver through holes!

Make sure you know how to read a map and if you are about to venture onto new territory, have a good look at the map to familiarise yourself with the layout of the land. You should know all the symbols used on the maps; if not, study the key.

Pay attention to the classification of roads and also the various lines used for electricity grids, pipelines and boundaries; these can easily be mixed up. Churches, Youth Hostels, telephone kiosks, milestones and bridges are all good landmarks and help to keep you on route during a rally. When studying new country, pay close attention to contour lines to get some idea of how hilly the country is: the heights of contours are written in the contour lines at intervals along their length. On Ordnance Survey maps they are printed so that they read facing uphill which provides a quick check as to the direction of the slope. Contours close together mean steep slopes and contours further apart mean more gentle ones.

To put the route of a rally on the map you should use a soft pencil (2B or 3B); never have a very sharp point as this may be difficult to erase. Always carry a lot of pencils – they keep breaking and have a habit of jumping out of your fingers and sliding under the seat at the most awkward moments. A small 'spring clip' pencil holder fixed to the dashboard or rear of the sunvisor is a good way of storing spare pencils.

Keep markings simple and never rub fingers over the map as the pencil lead quickly becomes ingrained and makes the map less clear for future occasions.

Road rallies have Competitive, Non-competitive and, sometimes, Special Time Recovery sections, so you will probably wish to use different markings for different sections. Some people favour solid pencil lines on both sides of the road on competitive sections while single lines on the left of the road indicate non-competitive sections, showing the direction of travel. It is usually best to draw a circle for a control.

There are no fixed rules, so please yourself – but keep it simple.

'Give-way' junctions, noise zones, no-lateness sections, non-competitive sections (where you must not make up time) must all be marked clearly. Mark where you change from one map to the other by writing in the margin "CM to . . ." with the number of the map you are moving onto.

Although you'll have time cards, roadbooks, regulations and so on in the car, the map is your working document and as much information as possible must be kept on it.

Always use a cardboard map board – never, never use metal, wood or anything hard because an accident can have very painful consequences if any unyielding board is rammed into your pelvis. The cardboard should be approximately 18 inches square and is purely used to hold all the maps in position. Some navigators clip them in position, others let them lie loose. A map board with rally information marked on it is helpful – information like average speeds, maximum and minimum times allowed etc. (one will be penalised for completing some sections in less than three-quarters of the official time). The equations for working out average speeds, lengths of sections, etc. are also useful.

A simple clipboard should be used as well with important rally documents like route and time cards etc., fixed to it. It is better to have time cards tightly clipped in position – marshals prefer something hard to rest on when signing your card. Incidentally, it is advisable to work out a routine for marshals; you may prefer to open the door and let them lean in. You can shine the light on the board for them and all of this saves time for you.

Always do your utmost to keep your time cards and other documents dry; a ball point will not write on wet, soggy cards and a felt-tip will make an unholy mess.

Occasionally on rallies you will be given small route check cards and these should be kept in a pouch or special envelope as it can be heartbreaking to discover the loss of a card when you have completed a long rally.

A map measurer (called an opisometer, consisting of a small wheel and dial) is useful to carry and a pocket calculator (for calculating times and average speeds) should be carried, ideally one with a built-in stop watch. Navigators should keep a close watch on silicone chip technology (electronic chips – not the Harry Ramsden variety!) because the dramatic advances in the last few years seem likely to continue and are making things easier for navigators.

Probably the most popular device for British navigators is the Terra Trip which is equipped with L.E.D. readout in red. The German Combi Counter and various models of Halda rally computers carry rheostats so that the brightness can be altered. Most of them will give you your average speed which can, of course be useful on longer road events and international rallies. Again, there are constant developments on this front so keep in touch with new models.

Many of the works teams make it possible for the navigator to 'zero' the digital trip meter by means of a foot-operated switch similar to an old fashioned dip switch or by a remote, hand-held switch.

These systems have obvious advantages when trip distances are incorporated in the notes which are being read on foggy sections. (More about pace notes later).

It is sometimes thought that the dashboard on the navigator's side of the car should be covered with dials and clocks so that it looks like a scaled down version of Concorde's cockpit. This is not true; like everything else to do with navigation it is better to follow the old adage of "keep things simple".

On a British road rally it is quite possible to succeed without any form of clock on the dashboard – a successful navigator may use his wrist watch (also a hand-held stop watch

The co-driver's side of the car must be neat and straightforward. This is a works Peugeot 309.

PLEASE NOTE IT TAKES A MINIMUM OF 24 HRS TO PROCESS YOUR CARNET. IF YOU REQUIRE THIS CARNET TO BE POSTED BACK PLEASE ENCLOSE A STAMPED ADDRESSED ENVELOPE.

ATA Carnet No.

ATA CARNET
APPLICATION FORM & UNDERTAKING

(This form must be typed)

To: The .... Chamber of Commerce and Industry

I, ... for and on behalf of

(name and address of firm) ....

Telephone No. .... Ext. ....

I am a member of the .... Chamber of Commerce, and my membership No. is ....

apply for a Carnet in the name(s) of ....
(give name(s) of accredited person(s) who will use the Carnet)

for use in the Following countries (please indicate the number of VISITS being made to each country and those countries being crossed in TRANSIT). Number of EXITS from the UK. ☐   (Yellow)

Visits (White)	Country	No of visits	Country	No of visits	Country	No of visits	Country	No of visits

Transits (Blue)	Country	No. of transits	Country	No. of transits	Country	No. of transits	Country	No. of transits

PLEASE NOTE:
YOU MAY NEED BLUE TRANSIT FORMS FOR FRANCE, ITALY & GREECE SO PLEASE ENSURE THAT YOU HAVE AT LEAST 2 PAIRS FOR EACH VISIT.

the Carnet is required for:

(a)   Commercial Samples

(b) ✱ International Trade Fair/Exhibition (please give name and place) ....

delete as appropriate

✱ Ensure that you have sufficient pairs of blue/transit vouchers as per fair/exhibition literature. e.g. Switzerland & France require 3 pairs of blues as well as 1 pair of whites.

(c)   Professional Equipment

IMPORTANT: The reverse side of this form MUST also be completed

Item No. No. d'ordre	Trade description of goods and marks and numbers, if any Désignation commerciale des marchandises et, le cas échéant, marques et numéros	Number Nombre	Weight or Quantity Poids ou quantité	Value Valeur *)	Country of origin Pays d'origine **)
1	2	3	4	5	6
1	Purpose built Rally support vehicle, VWLT Van with integral power supply. Chassis no.: Registered in UK No.	1		£6000.00	Germany (UK duty paid)
2	Trolley jack	2		£ 80.00	
3	Axle stands	4		£ 40.00	
4	Wheel braces	2		£ 4.00	
5	Fuel cans	8		£ 24.00	
6	Fuel funnel	1		£ 2.00	
7	Portapress	1		£ 75.00	
8	Welding kit	1		£ 30.00	
9	Electric wheel gun	2		£ 80.00	Germany (UK duty paid)
10	Electric drill with drills	1		£ 12.00	" "
11	Electric drill 90°	1		£ 12.00	" "
12	Electric grinder	1		£ 8.00	" "
13	Timing light	1		£ 12.00	
14	Volt meter	1		£ 5.00	
15	Comp gauge	1		£ 6.00	
16	Elopress bottles	2		£ 10.00	
17	Inspection lamps	2		£ 7.00	
18	Set taps & dies	1		£ 6.00	
19	Oil syringe	1		£ 4.00	
20	Torque wrench	2		£ 25.00	
21	Brake bleeding bottles	2		£ 2.00	
22	Soldering gun	1		£ 3.00	
23	Battery jump leads	1		£ 3.00	
24	Sledge hammer	1		£ 2.00	
25	Crow bar	1		£ 3.00	
26	Pair gloves	2		£ 2.00	
27	Silicone gun	1		£ 3.00	
28	Water carrier	1		£ 1.00	
29	Water bucket	1		£ 2.00	
30	Sponge	1		£ 1.00	
31	Leather	1		£ 2.00	
32	Tow rope	1		£ 2.00	
33	Torches	4		£ 4.00	
34	Elastic bungies	6		£ 6.00	
35	Track gauge	1		£ 8.00	
36	Tyre gauge	2		£ 6.00	
37	Air filter	4		£ 4.00	Germany (UK duty paid)
38	Oil filter	2		£ 6.50	" "
39	Injector	6		£ 12.00	" "
40	Injector pipes	6		£ 6.00	" "
41	Engine oil cooler	2		£ 12.50	" "
42	Engine gasket set	1		£ 15.00	" "
43	Injector pump set	2		£ 2.00	" "
44	Fan belt	3		£ 8.50	" "

Total Carried over / A reporter

The co-driver's role as 'office manager' may include responsibility for the 'Carnet de Passage' – in other words, the document which lets you get spares through Customs. This is almost as complicated as an homologation form and it will be the co-driver's job to complete it and have it stamped by a Chamber of Commerce. A 'loading list' will have to be attached to the carnet. Note that even sponges and wash leathers have to be itemised!

if there are any sections timed to the second) as well as just a navigator's light and a map magnifier.

Every rally car should really have a flexible navigator's light fitted. There are numerous makes and there are different lengths to choose from. Select one that will suit your car and will reach across the map, which will be on your knee. Some people mount the lights on the gearbox housing or on the door, although this may be a bad thing as the light can easily be knocked off.

The flexible light is used mostly for map work when the car is stationary but if it has to be used when the car is mobile use one with an adjustable shade over the bulb so that it doesn't dazzle the driver. Always carry a spare bulb. Some flexible lights are made with two levels of lighting – a white light for stationary map work and a red one for pace note use.

Keep all non-fixed items of equipment stored carefully and always in the same place, say in a door pocket or document case under the dashboard.

Maps, other than the ones you are using, should be kept in sequence and in a handy position. Another useful tip is to take a few extra maps of surrounding areas as you never know when you may have to go off route in the event of a diversion or retirement (or quite simply through getting lost!).

Some method of magnifying the map is

essential. There are illuminated magnifiers which work from batteries and while these are useful as spares they are not recommended for full time use as the batteries might run down at a crucial moment.

There are various illuminated map magnifiers on the market the most popular being the Don Barrow Light which has a built-in scale base (removable) a rheostat and powerful magnifying lens. Many top road rally crews even carry a complete spare light.

Most road rallies include sections of 'plot and bash', rally terminology for the art of plotting references whilst on the move. As mentioned previously a navigator can become quite adept at this and can gain extra advantage by using a hand-held map light containing a Romer base plate. This magnifies the map and the exact map reference point should be memorised, the light tilted, and spot marked in pencil and then double checked if necessary. It all sounds somewhat laborious but with a bit of practise a navigator can plot very quickly.

If you wear spectacles (many navigators do) remember to keep them in position with a cord at the back of the neck. Always carry a spare pair and consider plastic lenses – they are safer.

Your driver will probably expect you to be the bookworm! You should be the one to send for regulations and you should then study them very carefully. You must know what time you need to report for scrutineering, when and how the route will be given out, how much time you can make up, the difference between stage penalties and road marks, the penalties for lateness, etc. Many of these are very small points, but a mistake with any one of them could wreck your chances on an event.

When you get to the start of a rally the route you are given is obviously of vital importance, and so is any list of black-spots and 'out of bounds' areas which you must observe. Drivers are notorious for wandering off aimlessly during the preliminaries to the start of a rally, so find your man a particular job to keep him busy.

On many rallies you will find yourself plotting the route from map references, often with directions of approach and departure stipulated. Sometimes, particularly on smaller events, you may be given the route in more bizarre ways but if the rally is properly run this needn't throw you because no responsible organiser will risk the public nuisance of cars milling about lost because he was too smart in his route instructions.

Having progressed from navigational nightmares to very straightforward 'map reference only' instructions, road rallying appears to have gone full circle and, in order to curb the speed of competitors, road events have returned to 'plot and bash', regularity and other more devious methods of navigation. There are a few books specialising in rally navigation and it would be worth brushing up on the various different types of navigation. We have always advocated road rallying as the breeding ground for the future works co-driver. This is still the case.

Most crews incur 'fails' at some time in their career because of wrong directions of approach or departure. Always check these very thoroughly when they are stipulated and remember not to get west and east confused. You might think this is elementary but a great number of experienced competitors very easily confuse south-west with south-east and, needless to say, it is a favourite trick of organisers to place controls at junctions requiring an approach from one of these two directions.

Once you are under way on the event, keep your driver in touch with what is happening, but don't babble on too much; give him a chance to settle down, perhaps calling out the occasional phone box or something clearly visible to help him to build his confidence in you. When you are starting as a navigator, don't try to read every bend on the map to the driver because you will probably find that although you are making a very good job of it, you are actually on the wrong road!

Above all, concentrate (that word again!) on making sure that you are on the right road at all times, and that you guide your driver down the correct slots (turnings) without overshooting. When you can do this consistently well, start to call out the bad bends, then with experience you can start

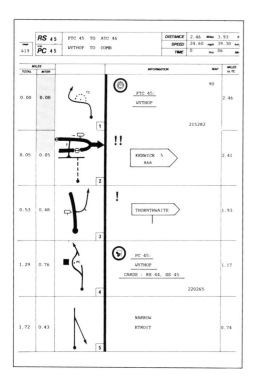

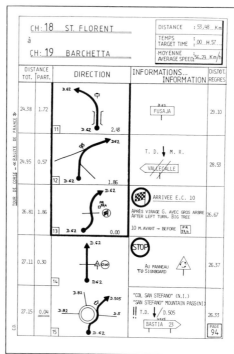

(Far left) A page from the roadbook of the Lombard RAC Rally. Both intermediate and cumulative mileage distances are shown. This section takes the route out of a forest, crosses a dual carriageway then visits a passage check before taking a hairpin junction. Note the map references of controls are given and important instructions are given in French.

◀ A page from the Tour de Corse road book.

. . . and the Rally of Portugal. Note that all World Championship rally roadbooks conform to a standard layout. The extreme right hand columns shows reducing mileages to the next control. ▼

◀ Route instructions American style, giving a detailed explanation of hazards. A water-bar is a point where the road crosses a stream, incidentally. This is a section of Arizona's Coronado Rally.

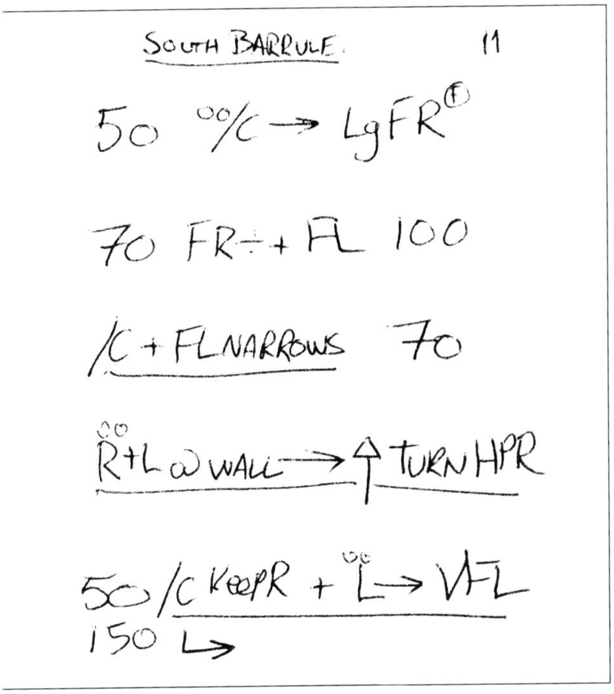

SOUTH BARRULE.   11

50 °%/C → LgFR ⓔ

70 FR÷+ FL 100

/C + FL NARROWS 70

°°
R+L ω WALL →↑ TURN HPR

50 /C KEEP R + °°L → VFL
150 L→

TRANSLATION

50 YDS ABSOLUTE OVER CREST INTO

LONG FAST RIGHT PLUS   70 YDS

FAST RIGHT MINUS AND FAST LEFT 100 YDS

CREST + FAST LEFT NARROWS   70 YDS

ABSOLUTE RIGHT AND ABSOLUTE LEFT AT WALL INTO

SIGN TURN HAIRPIN RIGHT   50 YDS

CREST KEEP RIGHT AND ABSOLUTE LEFT INTO

VERY FAST LEFT   150 YDS

---

ace notes are essential for a good performance on a non-secret route. These were prepared by Jimmy
IcRae and Ian Grindrod for a Manx International Rally. On the right we show how they would be read to the
river. When writing notes try to avoid starting successive lines with the same symbol or word – this
revents the wrong line being read.

---

nother example of pace notes – this time Ari Vatanen's. Notice how the notes of different drivers vary.

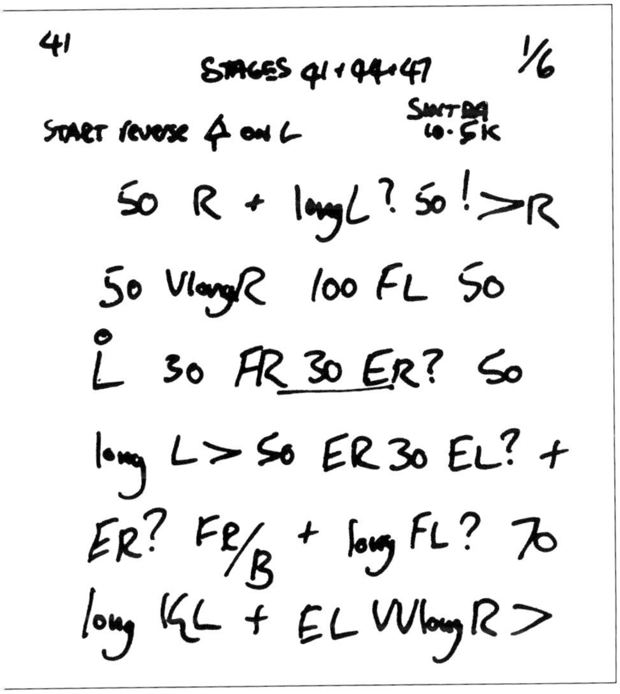

---

41   1/6
              STAGES 41+44+47
START reverse 4 on L   START DA
                              6.5k

   50 R + long L? 50 !>R

   50 V long R 100 FL 50

   °L 30 FR 30 ER? So

   long L> So ER 30 EL? +

   ER? FR/B + long FL? 70

   long KL + EL VV long R >

TRANSLATION

50 RIGHT AND LONG LEFT–MAYBE 50
CAUTION TIGHTENS RIGHT 50 VERY LONG
RIGHT 100 FLAT LEFT 50 ABSOLUTE
LEFT 30 FLAT RIGHT 30 EASY RIGHT–
MAYBE 50 LONG LEFT TIGHTENS 50 EASY
RIGHT 30 EASY LEFT–MAYBE AND
EASY RIGHT–MAYBE FLAT RIGHT OVER
BROW AND LONG FLAT LEFT–MAYBE
70 LONG K LEFT AND EASY LEFT
VERY, VERY LONG RIGHT TIGHTENS

to call out more gradual ones; how far you pursue this depends on just what information your driver needs. If he is inexperienced he'll probably be frightening himself so much that he won't be paying all that much attention to what you are saying anyway. If you have to return to plotting references and cannot assist the driver by reading the road to him, for goodness sake tell him, otherwise he might interpret your silence as an instruction to keep going in a straight line which could have disastrous results.

Marshals

Marshals are an important part of a rally; always be nice to them. Present your route card to them properly and hold your map light over your route card. Unless you have a lot of time in hand, don't get too involved in chatting to marshals as you may break your concentration. Try not to shout or argue with marshals as you are seldom likely to win; they have the upper hand! Some people still try to 'shout up' the time or bully marshals into giving them the time they want but most marshals have already been warned of this trick.

Make sure a marshal signs in the right place and check his work immediately. His is an arduous job and inevitably human error creeps in, particularly on a long, cold, wet night. Keep your road book clean if you can and if a marshal happens to make a mistake in entering a time or direction of approach then get him to scrub out the original entry completely, re-write the correct entry and initial or sign this alteration – it will be difficult to have things changed later. Don't let a marshal merely alter a figure as most rally regulations state that "any items on time cards that have been altered or appear to have been tampered with may be deemed not to have been made". You have been warned!

If you can, stay in the car at controls. Check your map work and time cards. Don't be eager to leave the car and blab your times to other competitors; they may be encouraged to try harder and pull back a deficit! We're talking about road rallying here, on stage events people keep a strict record of each other's times.

After a stop of any kind, remember to tell your driver what the next section is like – it is your fault if he sets off at half throttle when he ought to be pressing on.

We've talked about the importance of time-keeping – let's now mention the types of timing.

Timing

On most road rallies the marshals will hold the watches – usually clear, accurate, waterproof clocks or digital timepieces. Marshals will read off the time in hours and minutes, always reading to the previous minute e.g., 06 hour 37 mins 59 secs will read 06.37. On some competitive sections or on special tie-deciding parts, seconds may be used and the full time written in.

Where organisers use watches with hands (i.e. non-digital types) at controls where times are to be recorded to the second, the navigator should be wary of the most competent marshal giving a 'wrong minute'. For example, 22hrs 15min 58sec is easily mis-read as 22.16.58 because the minute hand is virtually on the sixteen.

Organisers will set and seal all timepieces to BBC time prior to the rally. These will be hired from companies who specialise in hiring out timekeeping equipment to motor clubs.

At one time competitors carried the watches used to record their progress but today only the smallest club rally provides competitors with 'sealed watches'. This system of timekeeping is open to abuse by competitors and marshals so is now never used on better events.

Stage rallies are always timed at normal time of day and the stages themselves are timed to the second or even fraction of a second. Generally speaking, the bigger the rally the better the time-pieces but all should be set by competent registered timekeepers. Printing clocks are also used occasionally.

The most common method of overall timing on a stage rally is 'Target Timing'. Quite simply, a target time is given for each road section in hours and minutes and you must not take less time than this or you will receive a heavy penalty. The system is designed to prevent speeding on the roads

2L opens -100

l1R down -150

!5L narr l2R -130 opens

1L -70 3L ↘ (1R +

4R → Turn early 5R)

2L - 30 AR/Cr - 30

early 2L - 50 1L - 30

3R-50 3L/Cr

TWO LEFT OPENS ONE HUNDRED,

LONG ONE RIGHT DOWN ONE FIFTY,

CAUTION FIVE LEFT NARROWS, LONG TWO RIGHT OPENS ONE THIRTY,

ONE LEFT SEVENTY THREE LEFT TIGHTENS INTO ONE RIGHT AND

FOUR RIGHT INTO TURN EARLY FIVE RIGHT,

TWO LEFT THIRTY, ABSOLUTE RIGHT OVER CREST THIRTY,

EARLY TWO LEFT FIFTY, ONE LEFT THIRTY

(THREE RIGHT FIFTY THREE LEFT OVER CREST)

David Llewellyn and Phil Short are among many who use a number system to grade bends. For example 0 = Open, 1 = Nearly Flat, 2 = Very Fast, 3 = Fast, 4 = Medium, 5 = 90°, 6 = Tighter than 90°. On the right we show how these notes from an Ulster Rally were read. Note the bottom right-hand corner shows the next instruction of the next page – to prevent turning over two pages at once.

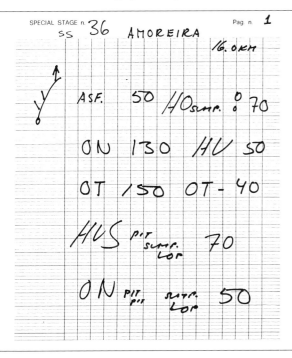

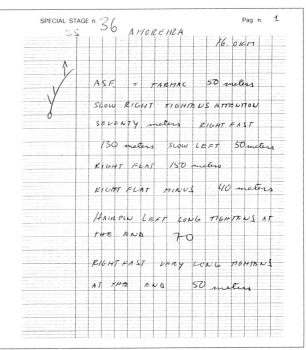

These are the notes of Markku Alén and Ilkka Kivimaki – one of the world's most successful crews ever. These are read in Finnish – they have been translated specially for this book.

after time lost on stages. Occasionally you will be allowed to book in at less than the target time but this is only likely to be at Rest Halts or maybe the Final Control but even then, you should never cover the distance in less than three quarters of the time allowed. This is the infamous 'three quarter time rule' and details are shown in the RACMSA year book and in rally regulations. You can be penalised for making up more time than this so don't do it. It's not worth it!

The time of arrival at the end of any road section depends entirely on the time you left the previous control. To calculate you simply add the target time for the section to the time of departure. Make sure you study the regulations for the event for there is often 'dead' time in between a Special Stage 'Arrival' and a Special Stage 'Start' control.

Although you cannot make up time, as a rule you are usually allowed to revert to normal at Main Time Controls or Rest Halts. Again, this will be made totally clear. If not, ask.

It's not as complicated as it sounds but it does need careful thought and, above all, make sure you totally understand the system before you start the event.

Another method of timing is 'Schedule Timing' where a scheduled time of theoretical car no 'O' is shown in the road book. To calculate your due time, merely add your competition number as shown in the following example:-

	Car 0	Car 1	Car 5	Car 45
TC 1	11.00	11.01	11.05	11.45
TC2	11.21	11.22	11.26	12.06
TC 3	11.43	11.44	11.48	12.28

It is normally possible to make up lost time providing you don't break the three-quarter rule.

Usually the maximum penalty-free lateness is 30 minutes but this will be specified in the regulations. It is also possible that extra delay allowance will be given by the organisers in the event of stage blockages or similar and the delays between a Special Stage 'Arrival' and a Special Stage 'Start' can also be taken into account. All this information will be published – if in doubt, ask the organisers.

At the end of a special stage a marshal will signal or phone through the precise moment that each car crosses the flying finish line to another marshal holding the watch at the stop line; cars stop at this

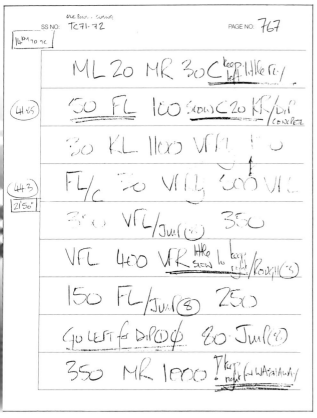

MEDIUM LEFT .... TWENTY .... MEDIUM RIGHT ....THIRTY ....
CREST KEEP LEFT LITTLE FLY .... FIFTY .... FAST LEFT ....
ONE HUNDRED .... SLOW CREST TWENTY KAY RIGHT OVER DIP
CONCRETE .... THIRTY .... KAY LEFT .... ELEVEN HUNDRED ....
VERY FAST RIGHT LONG .... ONE FIFTY .... FAST LEFT OVER CREST
.... THIRTY .... VERY FAST RIGHT LONG .... FIVE HUNDRED ....
VERY FAST LEFT .... THREE FIFTY VERY FAST LEFT OVER JUMP
EIGHT .... THREE FIFTY .... VERY FAST LEFT .... FOUR
HUNDRED .... VERY FAST RIGHT LITTLE SLOW TO KEEP RIGHT OVER
ROUGH THREE .... ONE FIFTY .... FAST LEFT OVER JUMP EIGHT ....
TWO FIFTY .... GO LEFT FOR DIP ONE UNSEEN .... EIGHTY ....
JUMP EIGHT .... THREE FIFTY MEDIUM RIGHT .... ONE THOUSAND ....
ATTENTION KEEP RIGHT FOR WASHAWAY.

Pace notes African variety. Even the Safari Rally is now a pace note event. These are the notes of Bjorn Waldegaard and Fred Gallagher. This is page No. 767 out of a total of no less than 849, which covered the entire event! No wonder co-drivers often suffer from sore throats. In the margin 44.3 shows distance from last control and 21'50" is the 'recce' time at this point.

marshal to have times recorded. The watch is sometimes kept at the 'flying finish' line and the time radioed to the stop line, but an organiser is better advised to adopt the former method in case there are any mis-read times and navigators ask to see the watch.

Going international

When you move on to International events, the navigator becomes even more of an office manager. You will need maps of course – quarter inch maps in the UK are close to the Michelins you will use on the Continent and will give you a feel for the scale – but there will be a lot more than maps to think about!

You will have to arrange insurance of all types, hotels, passports, visas (if any), boat tickets, maybe airline tickets, etc, etc, etc! And by the way, you will need a "Foreign Event Visa" from the RACMSA, which allows you to take part in overseas events – this is free.

Then you may have to organise fuel arrangements, service points – where and when brake pads should be renewed and

Although we don't profess to understand every word, you might wish to study Walter Rohrl's example of ice notes in German for the Monte Carlo Rally which he won. Added comments are made by ice note crews prior to the stage closing for non-rally traffic. These would be in coloured pen, of course.

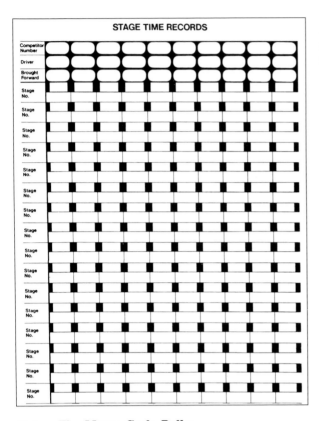

STAGE TIME RECORDS

Competitor Number										
Driver										
Brought Forward										
Stage No.										
Stage No.										
Stage No.										
Stage No.										
Stage No.										
Stage No.										
Stage No.										
Stage No.										
Stage No.										
Stage No.										
Stage No.										
Stage No.										
Stage No.										
Stage No.										
Stage No.										
Stage No.										

Left: **All co-drivers should keep a close eye on their rivals' times at every stage and will use a chart of similar design to this to record all the times. They'll probably obtain the times from the competitors themselves or from team personnel and will always verify the times on official bulletins.**

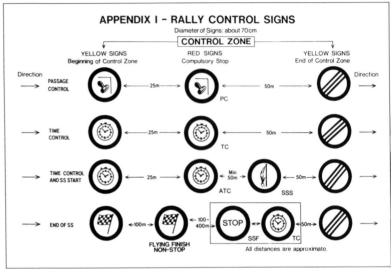

APPENDIX I – RALLY CONTROL SIGNS
Diameter of Signs: about 70cm

Above: **Self-explanatory international symbols for controls**

Below: **The Monte Carlo Rally organisers give route details in their regulations. This page shows the route for the Barcelona starters.**

ITINERARY : BARCELONE - E

Time and Passage Controls	Partial distances	Total distances
BARCELONE	0	0
Gironella (CP)		
PALS	279	279
Portbou (CP)		
Argelès s/Mer (CP)		
PERPIGNAN	146	425
Quillan (CP)		
Mirepoix (CP)		
Caraman (CP)		
TOULOUSE	210	635
Cassagnes-Bégonhès (CP)		
RODEZ	167	802
Aubrac (CP)		
Monistrol d'Allier (CP)		
Craponne s/Arzon (CP)		
MONTBRISON	282	1084
L'Étrat (CP)		
St Galmier		
SAINT-ÉTIENNE	46	1130

Michelin maps used for the routes in France :
Nºs 240 - 235 - 239.

4th Leg
FINAL LEG :
MONACO - MONACO
(100 cars maximum)

Communes	Routes	Distances partielles	totales

DÉPARTEMENTS DES ALPES-MARITIMES ET ALPES DE HAUTE PROVENCE

Mercredi 20 Janvier

25ème Secteur : " MONACO (Quai Albert 1er) - BIF. D 33 / D 2564 " :
15 km - Temps idéal : 0 h 30

	MONACO (Quai Albert 1er)			
	Bif. N 7 / D 37	N 7	4,60	4,60
Alpes	Éze-Village	N 7	3,80	8,40
Maritimes	Bif. N 7 / D 33	D 33	4,60	13,00
	BIF. D 33 / D 2564	D 2564	2,00	15,00

26ème Secteur : " BIF. D 33 / D 2564 - BIF. D 2564 / D 45 " : 10,00 km
Temps idéal : 0 h 30

	BIF. D 33 / D 2564	D 2564		
Alpes Maritimes	**BIF. D 2564 / D 45**	D 2564	10,00	10,00

27ème Secteur : " BIF. D 2564 / D 45 - BIF. D 53 / D22 " : 9,70 km
Temps idéal : 0 h 15

	BIF. D 2564 / D 45	D 2564		
	La Turbie	D 2564	1,00	1,00
Alpes	Bif. D 2564 / D 53	D 53		
Maritimes	**ST. MARTIN DE PEILLE**			
	BIF. D 53 / D 22	D 22	8,70	9,70

Carte Michelin Nº 245

Left: **The instructions are more detailed for the final leg in the French Alps.**

94

The entry form for the Rally of Portugal.

A page from the regulations for the Lombard RAC Rally.

Article 11 – Contd.

5. The Rally plates must be fixed to the front and rear of the car in a visible position for the duration of the rally.
In no case should they cover, even partially, the car's licence plates. Such an infringement shall result in a cash penalty of £50 for each plate covered (cf. Art.23).

6. The competition numbers supplied by the organisers must appear at least on both sides of the car during the whole rally. **They will measure 50cms×50cms approximately.**

7. If it is ascertained at any time during the event that:
   – any competition number or rally plate is missing a cash penalty of £50 will be imposed (cf. Art.23).
   – any two competition numbers or rally plates are missing at the same time, exclusion will be pronounced (cf.Art.23).

8. The names of the First Driver, his co-driver plus their national flags must appear on both sides of the front of the car. Any car failing to comply with this rule shall be subject to a cash penalty of £25 (cf.Art.23).

Article 12 – TIME CARD

1. At the start of the rally and at the start of each subsequent leg each crew will be given a book of time cards on which the times (Road Target Times) to cover distances between time controls will appear. Each crew is solely responsible for its time card.

2. The time card must be available for inspection on demand, especially at the control posts where it must be presented personally by a member of the crew for stamping.

3. Any correction or amendment made to the time card will result in exclusion from the event, unless such a correction or amendment has been made by the competent marshal and verified by his signature.

4. The absence of a stamp or official mark from any control or the failure to hand in the time card at each control (time, passage or regrouping) and/or at the arrival, will result in exclusion from the event.

5. The special stage sheets are an integral part of the time card and are subject to all the penalties laid out above.

6. The crew alone is responsible for submitting the time card at the different controls and for the accuracy of the entries and for the collection of time cards at the controls specified.

7. Therefore, it is up to the crew to submit its time card to the marshals in

so on. You will probably be in charge of planning service arrangements.

Realise that overseas events are not run on the same lines as British events – so don't assume domestic customs and practise necessarily apply – and it is important that you study the regulations carefully and make sure that you know what you can and cannot do without penalty. Ask the organisers and the more experienced competitors if you have any doubts whatsoever.

Be particularly careful about booking in at controls as many people have incurred 'early penalty' marks because they didn't study the regulations properly.

Don't forget to make sure you have all the necessary inoculations for the countries' you are visiting (making sure you have them in good time and have left the required space of time between injections). Don't become a sort of travelling pharmacy, but do take along the odd tablet for stomach upsets, diarrhoea, headaches and sunstroke; your doctor will advise you.

On most stage events and nearly all Internationals you will encounter 'Tulip arrows' because they are by far the simplest way of indicating a route. Tulip arrows are so-called because they were first used on the Dutch Tulip Rally many years ago – not because some of the diagrams look like tulips. Unless you have absolute faith in the organisers, plot a Tulip route on the maps then put the map numbers in the road book (the Lombard R.A.C. Rally does this for you), then even if you just use the road book you will be able to dig out the appropriate map if you hit problems.

If you make route or navigational notes Tulip arrows are by far the best way because you can easily and diagramatically

portray each junction. If you are contemplating doing a winter event, remember that snow might cover milestones and road markings, so only record items which will stand proud.

Pace notes play a prominent part in many International events and although you'll be well advised to steer clear of them in the earlier stages of your career you'll find them a necessary part of your life later on. Making pace notes and all forms or recceing is regarded by many as boring, futile and a complete waste of time. It's certainly very time and petrol-consuming but if other crews are using notes, you'll have to do likewise to stay competitive.

Pace notes are a way by which the co-driver can remind or tell the driver about the road they are approaching. Ideally the notes should be made by the crews themselves although it may be necessary to use notes made by other members of a team on occasions. This can be dangerous and there have been expensive accidents as a result of the misinterpretation of instructions perhaps because the terminology used by one crew differed from that used by another or because of illegible handwriting.

If pace notes have been made properly (preferably by several runs over the stage) they can be both fast and safe. Pace notes can be a great help to performance on a stage because they present a picture to the driver of the road which he cannot fully see; they help the driver to keep up the

Co-drivers rarely hit the headlines but these are among the best in the business.

Above, left: Ilkka Kivimaki (F

Above, middle: Juha Pironen (Finland)

Above, right: Luis Moya (Sp

Left: Nicky Grist (UK)

speed of the car and he should be able to position the car properly at all times.

If possible, pace notes should be finally checked at rally speeds, preferably in a rally car (initial note-making can be done in a much slower vehicle, say a hire car). It may help if a driver dictating notes relates them to the gears in which he will be travelling on the rally; this will keep his terminology constant.

A driver should dictate notes as he drives over a road to be used on the rally, giving the navigator the information he wants to hear later. The navigator should write the notes in pencil (which for some reason is easier to control) in large-style printing with only a few lines to a page and large line spaces.

Pocket tape recorders are not really a

good idea – you may put in too much detail and if they decide not to operate at a crucial moment you will have nothing to copy out. Put in various geographic notes (but not too many) as you will be able to keep your place better. Mention the odd signpost, house or sign, and keep your notes in a spiral bound book, written in black so that they can be photocopied and pages interchanged if necessary.

When re-checking the notes (remember, most crews will have as many runs over a stage as they possibly can) all modifications are also made in pencil and when the crew is satisfied that the notes are correct the navigator will write over them in a black felt-tip pen. All the background pencil markings and alterations can be removed with a soft eraser.

Some people write out notes in rough and re-copy them later but be careful, even the most proficient navigator runs the risk of missing out a symbol or even a line when re-writing, and if he doesn't have a chance to re-check the finished notes on the road itself he could be in big trouble on the actual rally.

The language used in pace notes must be clear and fully understood between driver and navigator. There is no standard language and many top crews have a system which is unique to them. Some people talk about bends in degrees (careful that degrees and speeds don't become confused), others talk about flat bends, easy bends, crests, etc. Avoid the use of words like 'slight' which could be confused with 'right'. 'K' is often used as this has a clear, unconfused sound but means the same thing as slight – derived from the idea that you are going up the arm of the 'K' (probably in second or third gear). Another popular method is to 'grade' the bends from 1 to 7.

Incidentally, you may find that your pace notes become over-complicated with involved instructions like "medium fast right maybe" or even longer phrases which are difficult for co-drivers to shout and quite impossible for drivers to absorb. If you watch rallies on TV with in-car cameras, you will find even the top crews falling into this trap – just make sure you "launder"

and simplify your note making system every so often.

A further sophistication of pace notes are ice and gravel notes which may be used on snowy, icy or gravel stages. Just prior to the passage of the rally an experienced crew will pass over the stage, marking conditions (such as patches of ice and snow) on copies of the notes – probably by underlining sections in red. These will then be passed to the team cars before they do the stage. Ice and gravel crews may also recommend the pattern of tyres to be used.

Lest all this talk of pace notes should confuse the beginner, let us remind one and all that pace notes are only used at a fairly advanced stage of rallying and only over roads where practising is allowed.

Any form of practice is usually strictly forbidden on a British forest rally although the Scottish and Lombard R.A.C. allow minimal reconnaissance of two slow runs over every stage. They also provide professionally made notes.

Under RACMSA regulations you may not mark anything on your maps unless it is information given by the organisers of the event on which you are competing. This should include route details and known danger spots and it is usually possible to follow the route on 1:50000 or 1:25000 maps.

If you are not provided with full information, the only way to know a stage route beforehand is by experience; most British forest stages feature the same route on every event and if a navigator is given the length of the stage he can probably work out where the route will go. None of this, of course, is much help other than to warn drivers of noted hazards. If you try to 'read' a forest track to a driver as you might a section on a road rally you will find it quite difficult at first.

Of course, if you follow the course through a forest on the map, in the event of a breakdown (or crash) you will at least know where you are. As navigator, it will be your job to walk for help (of course) and it is useful to spot that the stage finish is just a hundred metres away through the trees rather than following the arrows round the stage for ten miles! ■

A RALLY DIARY

You might be forgiven for thinking that in order to take part successfully in a rally you have only three simple steps to take:

1 Submit an entry to the organisers
2 Prepare the car
3 Get yourselves to the start by the appointed hour.

These three things must all be done, of course, but there are many more steps to be taken before, during and after an event before you can say your rallying is under control.

The purpose of this chapter is to try to place the more important steps in order so that you can see the areas to which you should devote attention at various times. Professional teams have – or should have – every item organised down to the last detail with comprehensive books of crew movements, timetables and schedules. This ensures that everything runs smoothly and avoids last minute panics.

A crew that arrives at the start within minutes of its starting time, or one which has spent half the previous night on the telephone trying to locate an elusive service crew, or one that has had a last minute panic to find maps or tyres, is just not going to perform as well on an event as a well-organised crew. So . . . get organised!

If the co-driver is doing his job properly, much of his duties will have been completed well before the start of the rally. In the case of private entries the driver will probably help in a lot of the pre-rally activities but for the purpose of this chapter let us assume that our co-driver is taking charge of all arrangements; we shall therefore address the reader in the role of co-driver. Although you will probably start on short events, near to where you live, we have covered a more elaborate event because the problems are greater.

So let us suppose that you are planning to enter a one-day stage rally in Britain some 150 miles from home. These are some of the steps you should take prior to the event. We have shown them in a diary form for ease of reference. Many of the suggested timings are approximate and you may disagree with them; there are no hard and fast rules.

Incidentally, as a driver or co-driver, it is advisable to make some sort of planned competition programme for a full year (this helps budgeting) and try to adhere to it as far as possible. Decide if you are going to tackle any local or major championships. Decide who does what before each event, so that you do not arrive in a town at midnight to find that you have no beds because each thought the other had made the bookings.

All of the following timings are calculated from the day of the rally.

Two months prior

Write for regulations – organisers addresses are usually given in the motoring press. Study the regulations and ensure that the car is suitable for the event (in terms of preparation and homologation). Be sure

YORK NATIONAL FOREST RALLY
SATURDAY MARCH 26th
123
promoted by YORK MOTOR CLUB LIMITED

**Adhesive rally plates are issued
to competitors on most rallies and should
be affixed prominently – front and rear.**

that the crew has (or can obtain) suitable grades of competition licence. Decide if the event slots readily into your programme – if it looks so costly that it will bust your budget or so tough that it may break your car then consider another rally instead.

As soon as possible after receiving the regulations

Submit entry forms to organisers together with team entry form and service crew request forms (if applicable) Send the appropriate fee, preferably by cheque.

Study the regulations to find the location of start, half way and finish, and decide how many (if any) hotel rooms you will require. Many rally organisers specify the hotel to be used as rally headquarters and often list other suitable hotels. Some even list hotel room rates and might include official booking forms with the regulations. It is quite common for organisers to negotiate special deals with hoteliers.

It helps the efficiency of a team if all personnel are housed at a convenient place prior to the rally. The most suitable hotels fill quickly – book early.

By the way, if all this sounds a bit grandiose and expensive, well, nobody should kid themselves that motor sport is cheap. However if the cost of hotels frightens you, try bed and breakfast places – or perhaps a caravan or tent.

If possible avoid driving a long way just before the start of a rally – you may save a lodging bill but you may not perform at 100% efficiency because of fatigue.

Try to discover from the regulations the types of stages and whether any practise is necessary or allowed (for the purpose of this exercise we will assume that there is no practise, therefore your entourage will travel to the rally just one day before the start). The organisers will probably advise you of stage surfaces; if there is any doubt from the regulations, telephone the organisers who may give you a little more information without actually revealing details of the route.

Discuss with your driver the mechanical and tyre requirements. Ensure that tyres of the right type are ordered. Have enough spare wheels.

Make sure that any parts needed for the car are available or ordered in good time and work out a car preparation programme. Some things are going to need

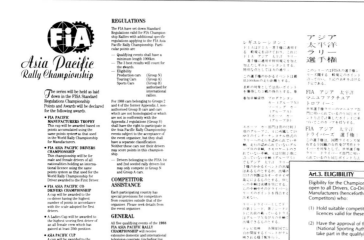

REGULATIONS

The FIA have set down Standard Regulations valid for FIA Championship Rallies with additional specific regulations applying to the FIA Asia Pacific Rally Championship. Particular points are

— Qualifying events shall have a minimum length 1000km.
— The 3 best results will count for the awards.
— Eligibility
Production cars   (Group N)
Touring cars   (Group A)
Sports Cars   (Group B)
authorised for international rallies.

For 1988 cars belonging to Groups 2 and 4 of the former Appendix J, non-authorised Group B cars and cars which are not homologated of which are not in conformity with the Appendix J regulations (Group S) shall have the right to participate in the Asia Pacific Rally Championship events subject to the acceptance of the event organiser, but they shall have a separate classification. Neither these cars nor their drivers may score points in this championship.

— Drivers belonging to the FISA 1st and 2nd seeded rally drivers list may only compete in Group N events.

COMPETITOR ASSISTANCE

Each participating country has special provisions for competitors from countries outside that of the organiser. Please seek details from the event organiser.

GENERAL

For all qualifying events of the **1988 FIA ASIA PACIFIC RALLY CHAMPIONSHIP** which receive extensive domestic and international television coverage (including live coverage). The events will be run in accordance to the 1988 FIA Rally Regulations. Non-homologated cars (Group S) and Group B cars of over 1600cc capacity are allowed to participate but shall not score points in the Championship.

FIA PACIFIC MANUFACTURERS TROPHY

This cup will be awarded based on points accumulated using the same points system as that used in the World Rally Championship for Manufacturers.

FIA ASIA PACIFIC DRIVERS CHAMPIONSHIP

This championship will be for male and female drivers of all nationalities holding an international licence using the same points system as that used for the World Rally Championship for Driver awarded to the First Driver.

FIA ASIA PACIFIC CO DRIVERS CHAMPIONSHIP

A cup will be awarded to the co-driver having the highest number of points in accordance with the scale set for drivers.

A Ladies Cup
will be awarded to the highest scoring first driver of an all female crew which has gained at least 20th position.

ASIA PACIFIC CUP

A cup will be awarded to the National Team scoring the highest number of points in accordance with the scale set down by the FIA for National Junior Teams. A maximum of 4 crews will constitute a National team. There is no minimum number.

The series will be held as laid down in the FISA Standard Regulations Championship. Points and Awards will be declared for the following awards.

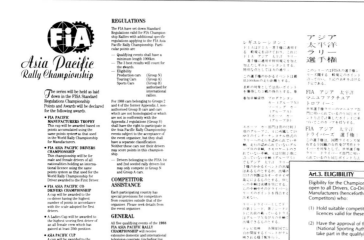

(Japanese translation column)

レギュレーション：
FIAはFIA選手権に適用する一般規定を設けているが、FIA アジア 太平洋 ラリー 選手権に適用する特別規定を加えたレギュレーションとする。特に気をつけねばならない点としては以下の通り。

この選手権のわかるイベントは最低1000kmの走行距離とする。
賞の対象としては上位3位までの順位の得点とする。

参加中核資格：プロダクションカー （グループN）
ツーリングカー （グループA）
スポーツ カー （グループB）

French and English are the 'official' language of world rallying but the organisers of the Asia Pacific Rally Championship give a Japanese translation.

These are pages from the British Open Rally Championship regulations – most championships publish their 'regs' in booklet form. ▼

Art. 3. ELIGIBILITY

Eligibility for the Championship is open to all Drivers, Co-Drivers and Manufacturers (henceforth called Competitors) who:

(1) Hold suitable competition licences valid for these events.

(2) Have the approval of their ASN (National Sporting Authority) to take part in the qualifying events.

(3) Drive a car listed in Art.5. and provide evidence of its eligibility on demand.

(4) Make available a nominated area on both front doors extending from the bottom of the window downward to the bottom of the door for the exclusive use of the organisers for the purpose of carrying:
a) The event identification number which will include advertising for the event and its sponsor, and:
b) the Championship identification logo (Art.3.5.)

(5) Display throughout each Championship event the Championship identification logo on both front doors adjacent to the top of the event identification number.

Art.4. REGISTRATION

(1) Competitors (except Co-Drivers) are required to Register for the Championship before the start of the first qualifying event that they enter.

(2) In applying for registration Competitors agree to be bound by these rules and agree to

display two Championship identification logos (Art.3.5.) on the car on all qualifying events. These logos are supplied by the promoters on registration and will be freely available at all Championship events or on request from the Championship Co-ordinators.
It is the Competitor's responsibility to ensure that he or she obtains them and that they are fixed on both doors of the car for the full duration of the event.
Any contender not complying with the requirement may be refused a start, or forfeit Shell Awards on that event. The decision to implement this requirement will rest with the Championship Co-ordinators.

(3) Once a Competitor's registration has been accepted it is not possible for him/her to disclaim any points for which he/she becomes eligible.

(4) Competitors and Manufacturers 5 scores will be used to calculate the final Championship positions (except as provided for in Art.1(2), and Art.8).

(5) Whilst entries for Drivers with FISA Rally Seedings will be accepted in Classes 1, 2, 3, 4, such Drivers will not be eligible for the PCD-OC (Art.6,4) Entries for Drivers with FISA Rally Seedings will not be accepted for Class 9.

(6) In competing for the Championship all Competitors must agree to be bound by these rules.

(7) A registration fee on Drivers and/ or on Manufacturers may be charged. Details will be confirmed in advance of the first event.

Art.5. VEHICLE CATEGORIES

(1) The Championships will be divided into the following groups and capacity classes:

Production Cars (1988 Rally – App 'J' Group N)
Class 1 — Up to and including 1300cc.
Class 2 — Over 1300cc, up to and including 1600cc.
Class 3 — Over 1600cc, up to and including 2000cc.
Class 4 — Over 2000cc.

Touring Cars (1988 Rally – App 'J' Group A)
Class 5 — Up to and including 1300cc.
Class 6 — Over 1300cc, up to and including 1600cc.
Class 7 — Over 1600cc, up to and including 2000cc.
Class 8 — Over 2000cc.

Sports cars (1988 – App 'J' Group B)
Class 9 — Up to and including 1600cc.

(2) Cars with forced induction will have their capacity increased by 70% to determine their Class Eligibility.

Art.6. SCORING

(1) Scoring will be divided into four categories. Competitors and Manufacturers will count their best 5 scores towards Final Championship positions, except as provided for in Art.1 (2), and Art.8.
Points are awarded to registered Competitors separately to each category as described.

(2) **Overall Drivers**
Points will be allocated to the registered Competitors according to their position in the General Classification from Classes 1-8 only and excluding all ineligible or unregistered cars and Drivers. The Championship will be awarded to the registered Competitors from Classes 1-8 inclusive who in accordance with these Championship Regulations has scored the highest points total.
Points will be allocated as follows:

General Classification of the Event (Classes 1-8 only)
1st placed contender   25 points
2nd placed contender   22 points
3rd placed contender   20 points
4th placed contender   19 points
5th placed contender   18 points
6th placed contender   17 points
and so on down to,
22nd placed contender   1 point

It is not necessary to be classified amongst the first 22 in the General Classification in order to score points.

Classes 1-9: Drivers.
A separate category based on the nine championship Classes (Art.5(1)).

Points will be awarded to the 10 highest placed contenders in each Class as follows:
1st placed contender   20 points
2nd placed contender   15 points
3rd placed contender   12 points
4th placed contender   10 points
5th placed contender   8 points
6th placed contender   6 points
7th placed contender   4 points
8th placed contender   3 points
9th placed contender   2 points
10th placed contender   1 point

---

replacing at given intervals – it makes sense to order them well in advance.

Sort out a service crew, though only if one is allowed. Make a detailed check list of the parts and tools they must carry – works service crews have detailed lists of everything down to the last washer. Don't forget the all-important fire extinguisher. Allow time for proper maintenance work to be carried out on the service car itself – it often gets forgotten.

Order Ordnance Survey maps for yourself and the service crew, as well as other small scale road maps for the service crew who will not need detailed maps for the whole route (petrol company maps are often quite adequate).

One or two weeks prior

Final instructions should arrive from the rally organisers; start chasing if you don't receive them. According to the event these instructions may include such information as additional maps needed, outline route details, as well as instructions about timing, stage arrowing and arrangements for service crews. Study these final regulations with great care.

Above all, the final regulations will tell you where to start, when to start and what time and where you must report for scrutineering. An entry list will be included and you will see the number allocated to

---

A page from the regulations of a typical one-day special stage rally.

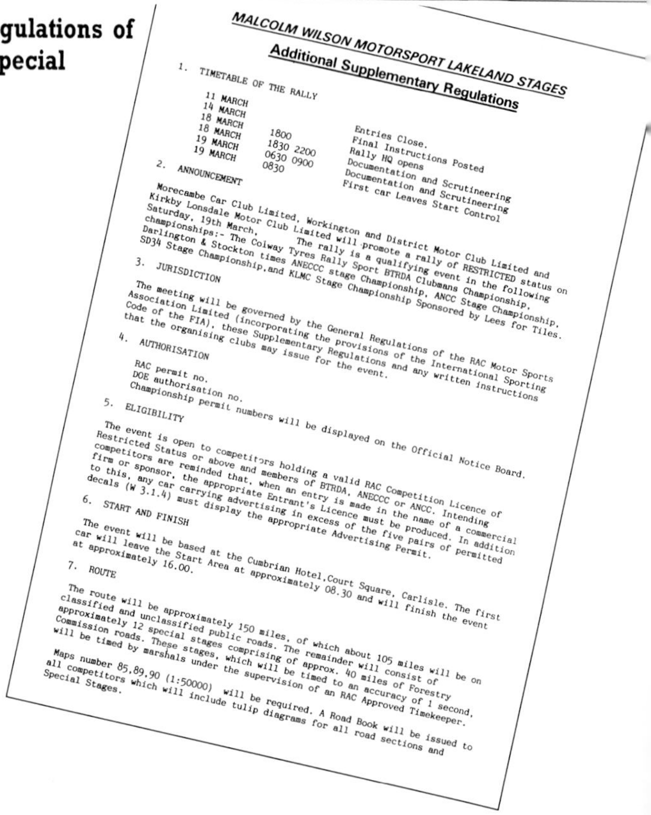

MALCOLM WILSON MOTORSPORT LAKELAND STAGES
Additional Supplementary Regulations

1. **TIMETABLE OF THE RALLY**

11 MARCH   Entries Close.
14 MARCH   Final Instructions Posted
18 MARCH   Rally HQ Opens
18 MARCH   1800   Documentation and Scrutineering
19 MARCH   1830 2200   Documentation and Scrutineering
19 MARCH   0630 0900
            0830   First car Leaves Start Control

2. **ANNOUNCEMENT**

Morecambe Car Club Limited, Workington and District Motor Club Limited and Kirkby Lonsdale Motor Club Limited will promote a rally of RESTRICTED status on Saturday, 19th March. The rally is a qualifying event in the following championships:- The Coiway Tyres Rally Sport BTRDA Clubmans Championship. Darlington & Stockton times ANECC stage Championship. ANCC Stage Championship. SD34 Stage Championship.and KLMC Stage Championship Sponsored by Lees for Tiles.

3. **JURISDICTION**

The meeting will be governed by the General Regulations of the RAC Motor Sports Association Limited (incorporating the provisions of the International Sporting Code of the FIA), these Supplementary Regulations and any written instructions that the organising clubs may issue for the event.

4. **AUTHORISATION**

RAC permit no.
DOE authorisation no.
Championship permit numbers will be displayed on the Official Notice Board.

5. **ELIGIBILITY**

The event is open to competitors holding a valid RAC Competition Licence of Restricted Status or above and members of BTRDA, ANECCC or ANCC. Intending competitors are reminded that, when an entry is made in the name of a commercial firm or sponsor, the appropriate Entrant's Licence must be produced. In addition to this, any car carrying advertising in excess of five pairs of permitted decals (W 3.1.4) must display the appropriate Advertising Permit.

6. **START AND FINISH**

The event will be based at the Cumbrian Hotel,Court Square, Carlisle. The first car will leave the Start Area at approximately 08.30 and will finish the event at approximately 16.00.

7. **ROUTE**

The route will be approximately 150 miles, of which about 105 miles will be on classified and unclassified public roads. The remainder will consist of approximately 12 special stages, comprising of approx. 40 miles of Forestry Commission roads. These stages, which will be timed to an accuracy of 1 second, will be timed by marshals under the supervision of an RAC Approved Timekeeper.
Maps number 85,89,90 (1:50000) will be required. A Road Book will be issued to all competitors which will include tulip diagrams for all road sections and Special Stages.

LAKELAND STAGES RALLY
ENTRY LIST

NO.	DRIVER/CO-DRIVER	CAR	CLUB	CLASS	CHAMP
1	Steve Bannister/Dave Oldfield (QUICKBITS, NOTTINGHAM)	Sierra 2100	Malton	D	
2	Don Milne/Neil Ewing	Metro 6R4 2999	Aberdeen	D	
3	Kenneth Dorans/Allan Burgess	Metro 6R4 2998	S&D	D	AD/AD
4	John Hepple/Jimmy Burns	Escort 1993	W&DMC	C	
5	Alec Cannon/Phil Sandham	Mazda 323 4x4	MCC		A/A
6	Jim Carty/Bobby Wallace	Metro 6R4 2998	LCC/EA	D	
7	Tony Stephenson/Peter Jackson	Escort G3 1995	FDMC	C	
8	Bill Lyburn / Allan Hutchinson (MORLEYS VIDEO CENTRE)	Ford Escort 1997	Ryton	C	
9	Steve Hunt/Gerald Clapham	Escort RS 2000	T/SH	D	A/A
10	Ian Joel/Gordon Capstick	Escort	KLMC		F/F
11	Bob Green/Mal Capstick	Escort RS 1600	KLMC	B	
12	John Morton/Alan Whittaker	Subaru FWD 1800	CDMC	C	
13	John Greves/Ian Jones (NAT WEST BANK MOTOR CLUB)	Escort RS 1997	BTRDA	D	A/A
14	Julian Adams/Richard Stamp	Escort RS 1998	Chester	D	A/A
15	Jon Ballinger/Reg Davies (HEREFORD MOTOR CLUB)	Manta 1997	Hereford	C	A/A
16	Mike Edgar/J. Dentice (CUMBRIA RALLY SCHOOL)	Metro 6R4 2998	EV	D	
17	Les Sharpe/Mick Smith (LES SHARPE ACCIDENT REPAIR SPECIALIST)	Sierra FWD 3400	DMC	D	A/A
18	Ray Cook/John Parker (COMPASS CARAVANS)	Escort 1593	Ty	B	D/D
19	Ken Skidmore/	Mazda 323 FWD			
20	Kevin Hinds/Dave Hill	Datsun 160J TC	KLMC	D	F
21	John Weir/Philip Birkett	Escort 2000	WDMC	C	
22	Andy Madge/Pat Cooper (A.M.E. PERFORMANCE PREPARATION)	Escort 1594	K&DCC	B	A/A
23	Nick Elliott/Simon Cresswell (CHELTENHAM MOTOR CLUB)	Escort 1993	ChMC	C	A/A
24	Richard Bradley/Sue Catlow	Chevette 2300	KLMC	D	EF/EF
25	Andrew Ludlam/Duncan Shaw	Ascona 2000	KLMC	C	AF/AF
26	Kevin R. Furber/Allan Cousey	Sierra 2800	BTRDA	D	
27	Richie Holfeld/Drexel Gillespie (HOLPACK PUMP SETS)	Metro 6R4 3000	TDC/MAMC	D	A/A
28	Ian Wilson/David Marshall	Kadett 2400	LCC/CCC	D	
29	Mike Stephenson/Julie Stephenson (JOHN WEATHERILL ELECTRONICS LTD)	Escort 1840	Malton	D	E/E
30	Trevor R. Pulford/Derek Staker (LEEDS MOTOR CLUB)	Escort RS 1598	Leeds	B	A/A
31	Ian Bell/Jimmy Carr	Escort 1600	WDMC	B	DE/DE
32	Kieron Patterson/Michael Wilson (SOUTH DERBYSHIRE MOTOR CLUB LTD)	Samba 1300	SDMC	A	A/A
33	Clifford Spencer/Andrew J. Bogg (FERTILIQUIDS)	Rover SD1 4200	BDMC/M	D	E/E
34	Mark Jasper/Alan Snell	Escort 1993	BTRDA	C	AC/AC
35	Phil Michaelides/Ralph Ahern (CHESS VALLEY MOTOR CLUB)	Escort RS 1993	CV	C	A/A
36	Ged O'Neill/Bob Berry (BULWELL AUTO SERVICES)	Lotus Sunbeam 2172	DMC	D	AE/AE

A typical entry form – this is for the Lakeland Stages Rally. ▲

◄ 'Runners and Riders' for the Lakeland Stages Rally. This list is sent to all competitors before the start.

Organisers of most rallies will ask for information to help the media and commentators. This is the 'age of sponsors and communications' so complete these forms sensibly – don't be flippant or try to be smart. This well presented form submitted to the organisers of the Skip Brown Rally helped John Leppard and his sponsors gain valuable local press coverage.

The good organiser will even issue a detailed plan of the start area showing where competitors should park. Local town plans will also be issued to help competitors find their way around the start. ▼

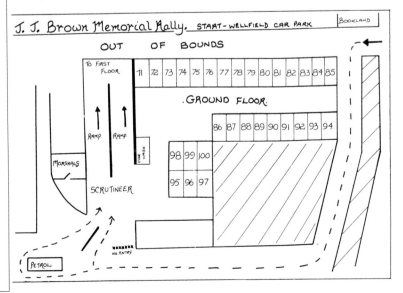

EAST BERKS MOTOR CLUB LTD OAKLEAF RALLY

SPECTATOR INFORMATION.

Once again the Oakleaf is here and hopefully it will be as troublefree as in previous years. However we rely on spectators to a great extent not to antagonise the general public as it is difficult for those not involved in the sport to differentiate between spectators and competing cars, so don't upset anybody, drive considerately and keep the noise down at spectator points. Some of these points are within earshot of peoples homes and bearing in mind that sound carries further at night don't shout to one another along the road.

Listed below there are nine spectator points. If you approach the spectator point as indicated from the nearest A or B road avoiding the roads so specified for rally use you should avoid the rally on minor roads.

We wish you a good nights spectating,

PR Officer, Oakleaf '78.

Grid Ref.	Car 1 Due approx	Spectators /pp.& Dept
165/872210G	23.10	West
165,152/ST 64 312 SE	23.35	North East
165,152/SU 74 0345 NNW	23.50	South West
152/ SU68 356 ENE	00.20	South
First Petrol- Please avoid Farthinghoe.		
152/ SP45 419W	01.15	South West, yellow to Brackley.
151/ SP514 487SW	01.30	North
151/ SP394 392SE	02.11	South West
Second Petrol- Radwells of Banbury.		
151/ SP306 425NEN	03.50	North
151/ SP42 048E	04.20	South

EAST BERKS MOTOR CLUB   OAKLEAF RALLY

STOP JUNCTIONS

```
A    765 190
B    690½ 190
C    673½ 154
D    653½ 198   ( also DIP headlights)
E    661 328½
F    710½ 317
G    757½ 332
H    765½ 335   ( also DIP headlights)
I    733½ 361½
J    615 349
K    613 332
L    557 357
M    529 362
N    518½ 439½
O    485 4554
P    490½ 488½
Q    444½ 474½
R    412½ 510
S    384 520
T    409 417
U    417½ 377
V    365½ 375½
W    261 404
X    285½ 373½
Y    355 349
Z
```

The following stop junctions coincide with Time controls. You will be deemed to have stopped at the junction as soon as you have been signed in.

```
648 226      574½ 330½      530½ 367½
316½ 404½    366½ 461½      430 435
370½ 378½    326½ 426       263½ 371½
362 302½     390½ 402
```

NOTE: DO NOT stop at the following junction.

```
                535½ 419X(Road conditions
                                permitting)
```

As stated in the final instructions 'Stop Controls' will be in operation at some stop junctions. These should be treated similarly to passage controls; however cars must come to a standstill as near as possible to the white give-way lines on the road and when signed in are free to drive straight off- provided nothing is coming of course! The procedure is the same at Time Controls sited at stop junctions. Other stop junctions will be observed in the usual way.

Road rallying has gone 'full circle'. The navigational nightmares of the Fifties gave way to more straightforward 'map reference only' events in general but the worsening problem of noise and disturbance caused the RACMSA to impose strict controls on this branch of the sport. So, over 30 years later the brain-teasing type of navigation returned, the aim being to slow down the pace of the cars. Will this stop the flow of top works co-drivers from Britain? Probably not, as an alert mind is the professional co-drivers greatest attribute. ►

Rallies attract spectators and it is important that they do not annoy non-enthusiasts – hence sheets like this.

A key sheet for the navigator to mark on his map.

Signing on is a vital part of every event. Make sure you have all the necessary licences and other appropriate documents with you.

NORTHAMPTON & DISTRICT CAR CLUB LTD
RAF MOTOR SPORTS ASSOCIATION
NEW CEDOS RALLY 1988

COMPETITIVE

Go from TC1 to TC2 via the following any order references:

663½313   656½305½
669½323   671½319½ STOP
647½312½   648½311½ STOP

NORTHAMPTON & DISTRICT CAR CLUB LTD
RAF MOTOR SPORTS ASSOCIATION
NEW CEDOS RALLY 1988

COMPETITIVE

TC2 is at SE 646½313½

Go from TC2 to TC3 via the following grid lines, references and spot heights:

64639319½32 STOP 64 STOP 64631273362

NORTHAMPTON & DISTRICT CAR CLUB LTD
RAF MOTOR SPORTS ASSOCIATION
NEW CEDOS RALLY 1988

COMPETITIVE

Go from TC4 to TC3 via the following: (coloured roads only)

STOP

NORTHAMPTON & DISTRICT CAR CLUB LTD
RAF MOTOR SPORTS ASSOCIATION
NEW CEDOS RALLY 1988

COMPETITIVE

TC4 is at 627½360   (coloured roads only)

Go from TC4 to TC5 via the following contour lines in order:

STOP 110 110 110 110 120 120 120 130 STOP 130 130

NORTHAMPTON & DISTRICT CAR CLUB LTD
RAF MOTOR SPORTS ASSOCIATION
NEW CEDOS RALLY 1988

COMPETITIVE

Go from TC5 to TC6 leaving every other grid square in the following
directions: (coloured roads only)

TC5 is at 646½380½, then: ESE   SSE   STOP   SE   SSW   STOP

NORTHAMPTON & DISTRICT CAR CLUB LTD
RAF MOTOR SPORTS ASSOCIATION
NEW CEDOS RALLY 1988

COMPETITIVE

Go from TC9 to TC7 leaving every junction in the following directions:

NNE   W   SSW   WNW   W   SW   SSE   TC8   S   E   ESE   SW   SSE   W   SW   SW   SW   TC7
          STOP   STOP   STOP STOP

NORTHAMPTON & DISTRICT CAR CLUB LTD
RAF MOTOR SPORTS ASSOCIATION
NEW CEDOS RALLY 1988

REGULARITY - Timed to the second, see Road Book 3 for schedule.

Go from TC9/RC9 at: 761 425½ NE,   to RC11/TC11 via the following
references, using coloured roads only:

76224264   77514153   78134303   78454297   79704452   80004450
STOP   STOP

To RC11 at 80504429

NORTHAMPTON & DISTRICT CAR CLUB LTD
RAF MOTOR SPORTS ASSOCIATION
NEW CEDOS RALLY 1988

COMPETITIVE

Go from TC18 to TC19 using coloured only via the following:

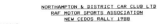

using the county boundary for 1.2 miles.

NORTHAMPTON & DISTRICT CAR CLUB LTD
RAF MOTOR SPORTS ASSOCIATION
NEW CEDOS RALLY 1988

COMPETITIVE

From TC11 at: 805 443 E,   go to TC12 via the following:

STOP

STOP

79   STOP

STOP at the next junction and QUIET to TC13 at 832 502 NW

NORTHAMPTON & DISTRICT CAR CLUB LTD
RAF MOTOR SPORTS ASSOCIATION
NEW CEDOS RALLY 1988

COMPETITIVE

Go from TC13 at: 832 502 NW,   to TC14 via the following ten-figure
map references in order:

8235050800, 8120050850 in unmarked layby, 8097550900 in unmarked
layby, 7970051250 in unmarked layby, 7952551250 STOP

7950051425 in unmarked layby, 7935051650 TC14 in unmarked layby.

NORTHAMPTON & DISTRICT CAR CLUB LTD
RAF MOTOR SPORTS ASSOCIATION
NEW CEDOS RALLY 1988

COMPETITIVE

Go from TC14 to TC15 via the following Roman Numerals, using coloured
roads only:

LII   LXXIX   CVII   LIII   LXXVIII   LIV   STOP at 2nd Junction

LXXVIII   LV   LVI   STOP XCVIII   LXXVIII   CIII   LVII

LXXVIII   STOP   CXII   LVII   STOP   XCVIII   LXXIX   LVI   to TC15

NORTHAMPTON & DISTRICT CAR CLUB LTD
RAF MOTOR SPORTS ASSOCIATION
NEW CEDOS RALLY 1988

COMPETITIVE

Go from TC16 at: 838 586 NNE,   to TC17 via the following, using
coloured roads only:

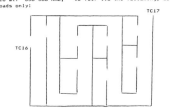

Clue: Draw your own herringbone. STOP at the 1st, 2nd, 5th and 10th
junctions.

NORTHAMPTON & DISTRICT CAR CLUB LTD
RAF MOTOR SPORTS ASSOCIATION
NEW CEDOS RALLY 1988

COMPETITIVE

Go from TC20 to TC21 via the following:

STOP at a point 49 Kms west of and 56 Kms north of 507½031½
Via   a point 63 Kms east of and 24 Kms south of 408½818
STOP at a point 81 Kms south of and 93 Kms west of 971 389 to:
TC21 at a point 33 Kms west of and 73 Kms south of NW 390½267½

NORTHAMPTON & DISTRICT CAR CLUB LTD
RAF MOTOR SPORTS ASSOCIATION
NEW CEDOS RALLY 1988

REGULARITY - to the second

From TC21/RC21 go via the shortest route through these spot heights:

11   NOISE CONTROL,   RC22 5 10 7 8 and 6 turn NNE to TC23/RC23

Here are examples of route instructions from the New Cedos Rally, a London Counties Championship event run in the South Midlands. The instructions for each section were printed on individual slips and handed to competitors en route.

	SERVICE 'A' TO SS 2		23.47 MILES	48 MINUTES
INTER MILES	TOTAL MILES	LOCALITY	DIAGRAM	INFORMATION
		SV 'A' IN		SV 'A' OUT	
		TARGET	0.10	TARGET	0.48
		SV 'A' OUT		SSA 2	
0.00	0.00	WEST SHORE		LEAVE SERVICE. RALLY TRAFFIC APPROACHING.
0.05	0.05			
0.08	0.11			PETROL
0.93	1.04	DEGANWY	30	POSSIBLE SPEED CHECK!
1.94	2.90	LLANDUDNO JUNCTION	30	
0.18	3.06	LLANDUDNO JUNCTION		SP CHESTER A55
1.15	4.23			SP BETWS-Y-COED A470
0.70	4.93	GLAN CONWY	30	
9.47	14.40	LLANRWST	30	

On a stage rally, navigation is much simpler. This is a page from the Gwynedd Rally road book.

your car. You will probably be given individual reporting times for scrutineering. Incidentally, if you don't like your starting number there is very little you can do about it. Don't ring the organisers bewailing the fact that your position is too low in the list and that you ought to be ahead of Fred Bloggs as you beat him in the last event. The organisers will be far too busy to listen to your twittering.

The driver must be told of any changes notified in the final regulations. Many people get caught out with things that have not been done through not noting changes. FIre extinguisher requirements, the permanent fixing of tip-forward driving seats, fire-proofing, spotlights, etc., are often mentioned in this context.

Let your driver know the salient details of the rally. Let him know the time that you and the service crew must leave home, and the time that it will take to get to the start. Distances of the rally etc., are also important. Don't fill his head with too much or else he will forget the more important points. As several people may be embroiled in your plans by this stage, it is worth giving them all a sheet with all the key information on it. If you haven't received confirmation of hotel bookings check with the hotel that all is in order. There is nothing like a rally for throwing hotel reservation desks into chaos.

Make sure that the car is beginning to look as though it will make the start line. Make sure that any parts which were expected to arrive have been delivered. If not, go for them or organise a courier service. Do not rely on British Rail or the post.

As soon as possible, your driver should be testing the car. He should be making sure that everything is to his liking. On the way to the start cover a few miles briskly on a quiet road to finally shake-down you and the car.

Day prior

Arrive in good time for scrutineering. Rally scrutineers sometimes tuck themselves away in back street garages which may be difficult to find. Make sure that the crash helmets are with the car for scrutineering (not in your hotel bedroom). Check if you have to report to Rally Headquarters within a specified time after leaving scrutineering. If so, keep an eye on this as you can be penalised for being late.

Go with your driver to signing on. Take your competition licences (and Entrant's licence if necessary) and anything else that final regulations ask you to show (possibly club membership cards or insurance certificates).

Collect road books, time cards or whatever else is issued. Collect service crew paperwork if required. Check that you have every page of every document as well as any amendment sheets. Have a look at rally noticeboards for any last-minute amendments, particularly route alterations. Not least during this process, establish who are the key members of the organising team in case you need to approach them later.

Now return to your hotel and plot the route on your maps. It is advisable to do this by yourself in perfect peace although some drivers help by reading out re-

TIME CARD 1	**MALCOLM WILSON** (motorsport) Ltd. **LAKELAND STAGES**						CAR NO.

CONTROL	TARGET	STAGE BOGEY	TIME			SIGN
			HRS	MINS	SECS	
MC1 Due	✕	✕			✕	
MC1 Actual	✕	✕			✕	
SS1 Arrival	50	✕				
SS1 Start _{Prev.Car}		✕				
SS1 Finish	4	1'55"				
SS2 Arrival	45	✕				
SS2 Start _{Prev.Car}		✕				
SS2 Finish	10	4'30"				
PC1	✕	✕			✕	

HAND IN THIS TIME CARD AT PC1.
ENSURE THAT MARSHAL ENTERS TIME FOR SS2 FINISH AT TOP OF TIME CARD 2.

Scrutineering Card		CAR NUMBER	
CHECK LIST		✓	
NOISE QA17	NOISE LEVEL 78 dB MAX.		Signature
BODY QA2	SHARP EDGES PROTECTED	Noise	
WORK	MUDGUARDS/SPATS	Scrutineer	
TYRES & QA9	TYRE TREAD DEPTH	Scrutineer	
WHEELS QA8	SPACERS & STUDS		
LIGHTING QH3	SPOTS CENTRE HEIGHT 24 In.	Club Card	
	SPOTS EDGE SPACING 350mm		
	SIDELIGHTS/FLASHERS	RAC Comp Licence	
	TAIL & STOP LIGHTS		
	NUMBER PLATE LIGHT	Insurance	
	REVERSE LIGHT/WARNING		
	DIPPING · SPOTS WITH HEADS	Signed on	
PASSENGER COMPARTMENT	QA7	STEERING PLAY	
	QA6	BRAKE PEDAL TRAVEL/H'BRAKE	Road Book
	QH4	RED WARNING TRIANGLE	Time Cards
	QA3	SEAT SECURE (Non-Tip)	Service
	QA13	FUEL LINES GUARDED	Road Book
	QA10	WATER LINES MARKED	DAMAGE AT START
	QH4(b)	WIPERS WASHERS HORN	
	QA2	PROTECTIVE BULKHEAD	
	QA14	BATTERY LEADS MARKED	
BONNET & BOOT		NO LOOSE FUEL CANS	
	QH2(c)	SPARE WHEEL SECURE	
	QH1	THROTTLE RETURN SPRING	
STAGE EVENTS	QH8	LAMINATED WINDSCREEN	
	QH10	C/HELMETS BS2495 (RAC sealed)	Continued overleaf
	QH7	FIRE EXTINGUISHER (S) – 5 Kg.	

A time card . . .   **. . . and a scrutineering card.**

ferences. When plotted, check everything and ensure that black spots, out-of-bounds areas and service points have been marked.

Now it will probably be your lot to plot the service crew's route too. Many people (including works teams) write a simple service schedule and hand the list of references and times to the service crew so that they can plot their own itinerary. Part of the fun of amateur servicing is that you almost take part in little rallies of your own – but don't let them get so carried away by their driving that they become a nuisance, either to the rally or to other motorists.

Always set a sensible average speed schedule for your service crew and don't forget to allow time for reloading a service vehicle after the rally car has gone through. Mechanics have been injured because of stupid service schedules – a heavily laden service car is not the best vehicle to drive quickly on twisty roads.

Make sure that your service stops are marked up in your own road book and on your map. The service crew must be advised of any out-of-bounds areas (organisers will often specify certain roads as prohibited to service crews to avoid

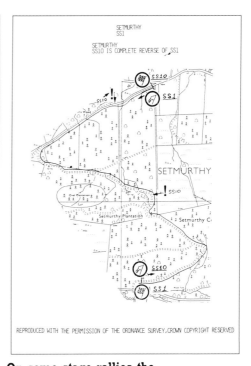

REPRODUCED WITH THE PERMISSION OF THE ORDNANCE SURVEY, CROWN COPYRIGHT RESERVED

On some stage rallies the organisers will provide maps of the stages in the road book. This forest stage on the Lakeland Stages was used twice, each in a different direction.

annoyance or congestion).

Allow time for a service meeting with your crew – you must check their maps. They need to know where and when you need tyres and fuel.

Incidentally, when leaving rally and service cars parked overnight make sure that as much as possible is locked away. Sadly, stuff does get pinched – even more ghoulishly, things get stolen from cars which have crashed and been abandoned on stages.

You and your service crew need to find time to eat before the rally but do not waste valuable plotting time on a four-course meal – order sandwiches and coffee in your room if there is any chance of running out of time.

Make sure your driver is not sampling the local brew too enthusiastically and tell him what time he has to get up. Try to send him to bed at a reasonable time and tell him to restrict any love-making sessions to about four hours! Service crews should also be told what time to book a call for.

Take another trip to Rally Headquarters just to make sure that there are no alterations. On an Italian San Remo Rally some years ago, the organisers changed the starting time and more than one experienced competitor appeared at the start when the rally had left!

Finally, book early morning calls and go to bed. But *always* take your own alarm clock. The chaos caused by rallies in the reservations areas can also spread to the early morning call department, as many competitors know to their cost.

Day of rally

Get up, get dressed (we'll spare you the ablutionary details) and collect together all necessary documents, ignition keys, crash helmets and if supplied (a very important item) the start card. Many organisers issue a start card at scrutineering which must be produced before you can start the rally.

Be at your car in good time, at least fifteen minutes before the start; many rally cars are the very devil to start on a cold, icy morning after a night in an exposed car park.

During the rally you should keep a detailed note of stage times together with other competitors' times. Don't blab too much to the other competitors but keep a running total of all the times and compare them with the organisers' whenever they publish a list. You will often find intermediate results displayed at main controls during the event. If these times and yours do not agree, do not get in too much of a tizzy as there are often mistakes in these results, which are usually telephoned through from Rally Headquarters and presented simply as a guide.

Apart from the usual navigational duties, (covered in detail elsewhere) allow yourself the luxury of a glance at the awards page in the regulations if you think you might be in with a chance, but this should be at a very late stage in the rally, probably on the run in. Many superstitious co-drivers refuse to look at that page until the car is locked up at the finish!

A good co-driver will be totalling his penalties on the run-in to the finish so that he is ready to check the totals when official results are announced. Make sure the car is left where it should be, i.e., in the finish compound; if there is any likelihood of winning a major or class award then it may have to be scrutineered for eligibility (this happens mostly on internationals).

When you re-enter the hotel/rally headquarters keep the driver away from the bar for a while – radio interviews with winners (well, you may have won) don't sound so good with slurred speech.

As soon as the results are announced you should check them with your records. Make sure they tally. If there is a figure with which you disagree you should check with the organisers to see if it is their mistake or yours. Stay within reach of the results room (stages are often cancelled or reinstated and this can alter the result dramatically). If your times do not agree, or if you do not agree with one of the organisers' decisions regarding a cancelled or reinstated stage, don't start shouting and protesting too readily. By all means, check with the organisers and make your point but study your case very carefully before considering protesting. If you feel very badly done

No	Driver / Navigator	Club	Cham	STC 4	STC 8	STC 14	STC 17	STC 19	1st Tot	STC 21	STC 30	Final
28	P SPENCER / I WOOLSEY			3.06	7.00	8.07	4.07	3.04	25.24	5.02	11.51	
29	NON-STARTER											
30	J ROBERTS	NON-STARTER										
35	NIL PIERCE / M WILLIAMS	NNCC / NNCC	A / A	3.47	6.50	9.13	3.35	2.57	26.22	5.01	12.33	
36	H EVANS / C M HUGHES	CAMC/NNCC / NNCC	-	3.03	5.27	6.59	3.19	2.10	20.58	RETIRED		
37	J H JORDAN / T JONES	CAMC / CAMC		4.50	7.48	13.12	4.49	4.04	34.43	7.19	F F	
38	A L SPENCER / R KENRICK	M WIRRAL / WALLASEY	A / A	3.51	5.24	6.34	3.11	2.35	21.35	7.38	8.37	
39	M ROYAL / I ORDFORD	CAMC / CAMB		RETIRED								
40	G EVANS / G BEER	HDMC / HDMC		3.38	7.53	RETIRED						
41	M BRODAY / S GRIFFITHS	PAN / PAN	D / D	4.07	7.28	10.12	4.11	3.43	29.41	5.20	15.53	
42	E BLACKWELL / E MARSHALL	NWCC / CVMC/NNCC		3.16	7.02	6.13	3.39	3.18	23.28	4.50	11.21	
43	S WILLIAMS / M HOLMES	CHESTER		3.30	12.00	7.06	3.11	2.59	25.46	5.50	12.45	
44	J G ROBERTS / I T THOMAS	BALA/NNCC / CVMC	AN	NON-STARTER								
45	P MOWLES / A ROE	CSMA / NNCC		3.43	11.01	7.26	3.20	6.03	31.33	5.17	12.03	
46	R JONES / S PUGH	TVMC		5.22	F	15.29	4.19	3.50	1F 29.00	7.32	F F	
47	M ATHERTON / J R JONES	HDMC / HDMC		RETIRED								
48	P KELSALL / A HAWKE	CHESTER / CHESTER	AWB / ANB	3.18	9.06	6.26	3.07	2.56	24.53	4.44	14.15	
49	S HASKINS / K HUGHES	NNCC / NNCC		3.48	7.30	10.59	11.21	3.46	37.24 F	F F F F	F	F F F F
50	C EVANS / N WILLIAMS	RHYL / RHYL		4.57	RETIRED							
51	I WILLIAMS / D ROBERTS	BALA/RHYL / BALA	A	4.28	8.34	RETIRED						
52	NON-STARTER											
53	Q CORNES / Q BELSHAM	ST HEL / ST HEL		4.56	7.38	9.53	4.57	3.37	30.41	5.18	F F	
54	H B WILLIAMS / A MARCHBANK	HDMC / CHESTER	A	4.03	7.03	12.51 F	3.46	3.20	1F 31.03	10.19	F	
55	G W WILLIAMS / A JONES	HDMC / HDMC	A	RETIRED								
56	P FEUTCH / E PRITCHARD	HDMC / HDMC		5.06	7.58	10.45	4.08	3.41	31.38	RETIRED		
57	T GROVES / K JONES	RHYL / RHYL	A	4.46	7.49	13.04	4.50	3.33	34.02	5.30	F F F	
58	G McQUILLING / I O'NEILL	NNCC/HDMC / HDMC	A	RETIRED								
59	N PARRY / H JONES	CAMC / CAMC		3.47	5.58	10.30	4.00	3.30	27.45	5.30	16.43	
60	M VAREY / P CRAVEN		D / b	4.53	7.39	9.54	6.38	4.06	33.10	6.40	17.53	
61	NON-STARTER											
62	J APPLETON	CAMC		4.36	8.16	17.37 F	4.42	F	2F 35.11	7.53	20.17	

The rally doesn't end at the finishing line – the results should be studied to see if the organisers' marks agree with yours – but DO NOT become a barrack room lawyer to win rallies by post-rally protests. Note 'F' = fail.

by, then you may feel you have to protest but please don't become a barrack room lawyer bickering and protesting about trivialities. The place to win rallies is in the car.

If you look like winning an award then make sure that you and your driver know where the presentation is to be held. Make sure that your driver goes to it; it is not unknown for winning drivers to be missing when awards are presented. This is the height of bad manners; you owe it to organisers, spectators, fellow competitors and marshals to be there. Dress as smartly as possible – no grubby overalls please. If you win, you will probably be expected to make a speech. Be succinct and genuine. You will not be expected to be witty or particularly eloquent, but obey some protocol – if there are Mayors, Lordships or whatever else present, then start your speech properly. Always thank the Club, the organisers and marshals, whatever your personal feelings. Never knock other competitors and try to appear as humble as possible without overdoing it.

Your work is now over, and you can let all those regulations, figures and numbers fade into oblivion. Until the next time, that is! ◼

HOW TO ORGANISE A RALLY

This chapter is included for two reasons: to give you an idea of what is involved in putting on an event (which should help you to better understand your part in the proceedings) and, with luck, to encourage you to take a hand in organising sometime. Organising a rally can be a thankless task at times but it can also be challenging as well as satisfying and, let's face it, the sport literally depends on those enthusiasts who are prepared to undertake the work.

One chapter in a book of this size can hardly offer a complete guide for organisers, but it can highlight most of the important steps to be taken when organising a rally. Remember, as the organiser of an average Restricted rally you will be catering for a hundred or more of the most agile minds in the sport, and they'll be ready to pounce on any small loophole that presents itself. So you must be on your toes from the moment you start to lay plans for a rally.

It would be unwise for a club to give the sole responsibility for organising an event to a complete beginner. Far more sensible to let a person gain experience by allowing him to understudy an established organiser before taking the reins himself.

Probably the first thing to look at from a club's point of view is the *reason* for running a rally, so a little self-analysis is no bad thing. Is the rally being run mainly for the club's own members? Or to try to swell club funds or put it on the map? Or . . . well it doesn't really matter what is the reason provided it has been thought through and the whole club is behind the rally – there is too much work involved to embark on an event without proper thought.

Having decided to run a rally, the club must decide whether to run a stage or road event. Numerous factors will have a bearing on the decision but the most likely will be the availability and type of terrain in which the club finds itself. Another guiding factor will be the relative popularity of the two types of event.

Although it must be the aim of every organiser to run a perfect rally with no mistakes, perfect events are few and far between. Even some of the world's major rallies make mistakes in regulations or paperwork. After all, there are a thousand-and-one things for an organiser of a rally to remember; nevertheless, every organiser should strive for perfection.

A club will need a small team or committee of people to organise an event, the size of the team depending on the size and nature of the rally. Generally speaking, stage rallies require greater manpower and are probably more difficult for the beginner to organise although the organiser of a road rally may meet his share of problems during the route authorisation stage, unless he is very lucky.

However, assuming that you are going to organise a road rally, fix the date and duration of the event. Selecting the date can be difficult; it is no good running a rally if it is going to clash with another event the same night. If the route clashes in the same area then you will not be able to run your rally, and if the event clashes with one in a different area, then you will probably not attract entries. So great care must be taken in selecting a suitable date.

It will be necessary to apply for a date through your local Regional Association's "dates meeting". Most of the better established rallies have a traditional date, so if you plan to use the same area keep away from their dates. You must keep six weeks away from any club running in your patch.

Naturally an organiser must have a good idea of the time of year he plans to run the rally. Some of the factors that might influence a date choice are the hours of darkness at a given time of year, the condition of unsurfaced tracks during different seasons or any regional peculiarities, like the presence of holiday-makers.

At a very early stage you will have to decide on the area in which you plan to run the rally, bearing in mind most of the best rally territory is already well spoken for. It is best to run a rally in your own area if possible as this makes the marshalling and route work much easier and, in any case, clubs in other areas won't thank you if you invade their area and upset the natives, the police or anyone else.

Among all the other decisions to be made at an early stage will be that of the status of the event. Obviously, novice organisers should start off on twelve car or "closed-to-club" rallies while an experienced team should be able to cope with a 'clubman-eight' or Restricted/Regional event. Generally speaking, the bigger the event, the better the standard of entry and therefore the more demanding and critical their requirements.

No rally can be run legally unless the event is 'approved'. The only events that do not have to conform to the Motor Vehicles (Competition and Trials) Regulations, 1969, are 1) events with not more than twelve vehicles, 2) events where there is no route and where competitors are not timed or required to visit places other than a finish venue, 3) road safety events and. 4) military training exercises (we know some rally cars are built like tanks – some even handle like them – but they still don't fall into this category).

However, the R.A.C. Motor Sports Association will need details of even a twelve car event before waiving the need for a permit and such events must be classified as either navigational, economy or vintage (veteran) on the application form to them. Note that road twelve car rallies which do not fit in any of the above categories are not allowed. No twelve car rally must be scheduled to run between 18.00 hours on a Saturday and 07.00 on a Sunday and, quite rightly, a prescribed amount of P.R. work is necessary. Details of the route must be supplied to the Route Liaison Officers who we'll talk about in a moment.

Assuming that your event requires authorisation then it will be necessary for you to study the statutory regulations and complete the appropriate application forms. These are available from the R.A.C. Motor Sports Association Ltd,. Motor Sports House, Riverside Park, Colnbrook, Slough SL3 OH6 (0753 681736) and from the Royal Scottish Automobile Club, 11 Blythswood Square, Glasgow (041-221-3850).

APPLICATION FOR A PERMIT

Name of Organising Club(s).......................

Date of Event .... Date of Practice (if different) ....
Status of Event .... Venue ....

The above club(s) applies for a Permit to organise the following event, which will be held under the General Regulations of the RAC Motor Sports Association Ltd (incorporating the provisions of the International Sporting Code of the FISA), any subsequent requirements of the RAC MSA and the Supplementary Regulations overleaf.

TYPE OF EVENT:
(please tick appropriate boxes)

CAR RACE R	SPEED S	OFF-ROAD X	KART RACE K
	Sprint	Autocross	Kart Circuit
	Hill Climb	Rallycross	Long Circuit
	Drag Race	Grass Track	
	Sand Race	2CV/Minicross	
		Stock Car Race	

RALLY Y	TRIAL T	AUTOTEST A	CROSS COUNTRY C
Road	Sporting		Trial
Navigation	Production		Safari
Economy	Classic		Hill Rally
Vintage			Timed Trial
Stage			Orienteering
Single Venue			Team/Winch
Road 12 Car			Recovery

In the following form, please complete all sections indicated by the **code letter** for the type of event being organised plus all sections which have no code letter.

Secretary of the Meeting
Name...................... Signature......................
Address...................... Date......................
....
....
Phone (Day) .... (Evening)......................

SUPPLEMENTARY REGULATIONS

...tary Regulations issued to competitors must be exactly in accordance with those shown below, in either wording or order.

...s in the sections appropriate to the type of event should be completed using block capitals or

...wn in bold type, e.g. **being sponsored by**, should be deleted if inapplicable.

...wn in brackets, e.g. (L2.5) are for information and should NOT appear in the printed S.R.'s.

...t may be submitted if there is insufficient room to answer any specific question.

...tion is only applicable to a specific type of event(s) this is indicated by underlining e.g. Rallies.

...must comply with Sections D11.2 & D11.3 in the Motor Sports Year Book.

SUPPLEMENTARY REGULATIONS

......................Club(s)
......................(status) permit ....(type of event)
......at ....(venue or start venue)

...vill be governed by the General Regulations of the RAC Motor Sports Association Ltd., ...he provisions of the International Sporting Code of the FISA), these Supplementary Regulations ...instructions that the organising club may issue for the event.

...it Number......................(this will be supplied with the Permit Advice Note) has been issued.
...ation Number......................(or D.O.E. Authorisation has been applied for). Rallies. only.

...n to:
...cted members of the organising club.
...of the following clubs, (or championships, or associations) (D3.1.3)

...itors holding a valid RAC MSA National or International Competition Licence. (Autotest and ...RAC MSA licence)
...itors holding: a valid International Competition Licence.
...pplies for Closed events, 4(a) and 4(b) for Clubman and Restricted, 4(c) for National and 4(d) ...ional events.

...and drivers must produce a valid **Competition Licence, Medical Certificate, Club Membership ...ship Registration Card** (delete as appropriate).

...und of the ....championship(s)
...of the meeting will be:–
...arts at ....**Individual times for scrutineering will be notified in Final Instructions.**
...not signed on by......................may be excluded
...at
...first race will be at ....
...rt Race Meetings. There will be......................races as follows:
...ach race, classes or formulae, whether heats and final, handicap races etc).

(a) All vehicles must comply with RAC MSA Technical Regulations or Kart Technical Regulations (for events up to National Status).
(b) Competitors in races number......................**must produce Homologation forms at Scrutineering and have them available throughout the meeting.**

Organising a rally is a demanding business. Here are just two pages of the application form for a rally permit.

Before submitting the application and route for authorisation you must make contact with numerous organisations. The Regional Associations of Car Clubs play a useful role in co-ordinating lists of road information and can often save many wasted hours by giving advice on certain areas to avoid; putting your route through some of these areas can mean almost certain refusal from the rally authorisation department.

Each County or Police area has a Route Liaison Officer and he has full information available to prevent rally problems. These people have various Police areas and National Parks areas assigned to them and they will make all the necessary contacts initially. They will also advise you.

Organisers of events planning to use British forests should contact the RACMSA's Forestry Liaison Officer for the area. These unpaid enthusiasts have great knowledge of the working of the forests within their area and clubs must channel all their enquiries through them – not to the Forestry Commission direct.

From the above you will probably gather that the RACMSA is doing everything in its power to keep the peace between rallyists and the authorities. They are generally successful but there are some areas in Britain (and the rest of the world) where rallies are far from welcome.

Anyway, after the informal approaches have been cleared, you are ready to submit your application for authorisation. Read Schedule 3 of the Statutory Regulations to make sure that your event complies fully with them. There are seventeen separate standard conditions which the event must fulfil, most of which concern the routing and timing of the event. If the event does not comply with the standard conditions then the organiser and competitors can face a fine of £50 under Section 15 of the Road Traffic Act 1972.

When the application form is sent in to the authority, two copies of a tracing from the appropriate 1:50,000 scale Ordnance Survey map (quarter inch O.S. map in the case of Scotland) must also be submitted. The tracings must contain full details of the route together with details of timing and controls.

It may seem unnecessary to submit an application six months before an event but it can take a long time to gain authorisation, particularly if there are any route clashes when the R.A.C. will suggest re-routes and tracings will fly back and forth between authorisers and organisers.

It will be necessary to pay an authorisation fee should your event be given the green light. This is based on the number of vehicles taking part and upon the length of event. It can range from £1.40 to £5.60 per vehicle. An RACMSA recognised club will also require an RACMSA permit. Once a club is recognised by the RACMSA it agrees to be bound by rules and regulations that are laid down in the R.A.C. Motorsport Regulations and updated each year in their Year Book. The Year Book deals with all forms of motor sport and has a section purely devoted to rallies where requirements and standard conditions are laid down. The RACMSA permit provides Third Party legal liability insurance and should be applied for some six weeks or so

before the event. The fees for this are again based on a per capita basis.

Talking about insurance, remember that most private insurance policies no longer give cover for rallies and so the RACMSA's brokers have devised a scheme whereby individuals can obtain road traffic cover for the duration of an event. The administration of this insurance must be done through the organising club and the brokers issue a block cover note for the event. The RACMSA will give details of this insurance, together with another policy which insures officials during an event (providing they have all signed a special form).

In the previous paragraphs we have implied that the event to be organised is a road rally; certainly these can be more complicated in the authorisation application stages. Similar procedures will have to be followed by the organisers of a stage rally although there will, of course, need to be more liaison with individual land-owners. Permission from land-owners will have to be submitted to the authorisation department and it will be necessary to obtain land-owners' indemnity insurance, as well as the other insurances.

As mentioned earlier, an organising club

Without marshals there would be no rallying. Here a stalwart signs on for a hard night's work in Herefordshire. Note the pre-set clocks, envelopes containing marshals' instructions and control signs which will all be issued.

Scrutineering will often be more for safety than homologation purposes. Here a scrutineer checks helmets . . .

. . . tyre condition and wheel bearings

. . . and seat mountings. Lights will also be checked before a night rally.

will need to form a small team or committee to organise a rally. This committee should have a chairman who should establish general principles and make the major decisions; ideally he should be experienced in rallying, either as organiser or competitor. However, perhaps the most important post is that of Clerk of the Course who will be responsible for route-finding, together with the time schedules and general layout of the event. The Secretary of the Meeting will be responsible for most of the paperwork – production of regulations and so on – as well as for administration during the event and maybe the results team too. An Entry Secretary is a useful addition to the team as he can take one onerous chore away from the Secretary.

A number of co-ordinators, or sector marshals should be appointed; they will look after certain sections of the route and be able to make emergency decisions in their area on the day of the rally.

In the case of a stage rally a Commander should be appointed for each stage to take control of that section – his counterpart in road rallies will be in charge of a group of controls; great experience is necessary for these people as they can make or mar an event.

A Public Relations Officer is most important as he is the person who makes written and personal contact with many of the people who may well be opposed to the rally. He will need a lot of assistance and ideally lead a team of articulate, knowledgeable (and tactful!) people who will attempt to iron out any route-finding P.R. problems at an early stage, by calling on land-owners and householders before (and in some cases after) the event.

Much of the work takes place before the event but on the day or night of the rally it will be absolutely essential to have another important person, the Results Marshal. He should head a team organised to produce speedy, accurate results – these will probably be fed in from various sections of the route by telephone and confirmed by completed documents as the rally progresses.

Naturally, computers can be used in the calculation of results and of course are frequently used for the major rallies, but beware. Unless you have a professional programmer and operator involved steer well clear of computers, for a few wrongly applied penalties can soon have the opposite effect to speeding up the results!

Other posts which are important though the level may vary according to the size of the event, are Medical Officer, Chief Safety Officer, Programme Officer, Chief Timekeeper and Equipment Officer. All events will also require a Scrutineer and Stewards and these people must be fully qualified and fully acquainted with their duties; don't just appoint people under the Old Pals Act. Note that there should be enough scrutineers to avoid queues building up.

Organisers of special stage rallies will need to pay particular attention to medical aspects and in addition to the Chief Medical Officer other medically qualified people should be available and positioned properly. Accidents happen and a stage rally organiser must cover every detail so that any accidents can be dealt with efficiently. Doctors, ambulances, fire appliances and breakdown teams must be available to get to any section quickly and everybody must be aware of the various channels of communication.

Having planned everything in the utmost detail before the event the rally organiser must then be prepared for numerous last-minute changes. Many rally organisers have suddenly found sections of their route impassible because of floods, ice, snow or fallen trees, and competent people must be available to make re-routes and support

All cars will have to pass a rigid noise check before and often during every type of rally. Here a marshal uses an approved decibel meter.

them with written documentation literally minutes before the arrival of the first car.

Incidentally. It makes sense to have someone delegated to promote the event and get publicity for it – if sponsors are involved they may be able to help here. They must liaise with local newspapers and radio stations by supplying them with details of interesting entries, etc. They will not only be carrying out a valuable P.R. service for your club and your event, but also for rallying as a whole. They must liaise with any local civic dignitary or a celebrity who may be called upon to start the event. In addition they may get involved with the printing of the programmes and a number of very important details which contribute towards the success of an event.

Try not to combine the media promotion with the task of doing P.R. with farmers and householders along the route: they are different jobs. Both are important and need individual attention.

Now let us consider the rally documents. All road books, route cards, time cards and other printed matter must be of high quality, easily read and understood. Be particularly clear and concise in wording instructions and let there be no excuse for misunderstandings. We apprieciate that not all rally budgets will run to beautifully printed documents but ordinary duplicating or Xerox prints will be quite satisfactory, just make sure that every sheet handed out is totally readable. If you have a club badge or "house style" then try to ensure that this is featured in all your printed material.

The chapter on rally navigation covered the different types of route instruction; a straightforward list of map references, with directions of approach and/or departure will probably form the basis of a road rally. Incidentally, check everything that is printed – a small printer's error could produce absolute chaos with your entire rally entry bogged down in a field!

For special stage rallies the route should be given out in the form of a Tulip road book. Some organisers think that this is not totally necessary and that a few map references will suffice but when competitors are required to visit some stages more than once confusion can easily be caused by the navigator having too many lines on his map. Tulip arrows are simple to prepare and simple to read. Organisers will probably need to make at least two complete trips round the route to collect all the junction diagrams, distances and signpost directions. All junctions and mileages should be put into order and clearly typed, preferably with a clear faced typewriter. The road book must give the competitor all the information for him to complete the route. Like everything else in rallying, the clearer and simpler the better.

In addition to the route, the road book should contain details of relevant telephone numbers, list of controls and special stages, service and rest halts and any other useful information. Procedure at special stages should be reiterated and there should also be special notes about damage, and indeed a damage declaration form, as this will enable any route damage to be traced by the organisers, providing a form has been returned to them.

The marking of special stages is a topic that causes great discussion wherever rally crews meet, but again, the most sensible guideline is to make sure that everything is marked clearly and without ambiguity. The RACMSA demand that a 'Tulip' route map or diagram of every stage should be given to competitors and that all junctions are clearly arrowed, unused roads being blocked off by logs or tape.

Advance arrows should be placed approximately 50 yards before a junction (or fire break), but if competitors are likely to be travelling at really high speeds the distance should be increased to give adequate braking distance before the corner.

Arrows on junctions should be placed either side of the road to form a 'gate' through which competitors will pass (be sure to leave them far enough apart so that they do not get knocked over). The arrows should always show the general direction of the exit road using one of the following positions: straight on, 45° right or left, 90° right or left and 135° right or left. It is important that the advance arrows and the arrows on the junctions are identical in the direction in which they point. As mentioned, any road that is not being used must be physically blocked off and a "no entry" sign placed several metres into the road in case somebody goes along it by mistake.

When signposting airfields take particular care to make sure the route is as clear as possible as the number of stories of people lost on airfield stages over the years would fill a book twice this size. One little arrow leaning against a straw bale in the centre of a mile-long runway will not be easily picked up on a wet and windy night!

Caution boards are important and should be used by responsible rally organisers, though not over-used. Some organisers take the view that "all's fair in love and war" and seem to derive satisfaction from seeing expensive cars drop over rocky ledges. Better organisers will place a caution board where there is an obvious chance that accidents will occur and only the most foolish drivers will ignore such boards.

While on the subject of boards let us mention that flying finish and finish-line boards should be positioned intelligently so that cars have enough room to slow down and stop between a flying finish and the stop line. For International events these boards must be in pairs, positioned on each side of the track.

When a stage has been arrowed and fully set up, at least two cars should travel over the route. One should be driven at a fairly slow speed in order to double check that all is correct and the other should be driven at rally speed to give a competitor's view of things.

Morecambe Car Club Ltd
A member of the Association of Northern Car Clubs and the Association of North East & Cumbria Car Clubs

Please reply to:

S. Lawrenson,
Bell Cottage,
Burton-in-Kendal,
Carnforth,
TEL. (.1.) 7816?

MORECAMBE CAR CLUB LTD.

ILLUMINATIONS RALLY 19/20 FEBRUARY

This Rally is promoted by the above Club under the rules and guidance of the Royal Automobile Club. The route of approximately 200 miles has been approved by the R.A.C. and consequently, permission to run the Rally on this date has been granted by the Depratment of the Environment. The local Police Authorities, National Park Board and National Farmers Union also have been informed of the passage of this event.

We have attempted in the planning of the route to avoid most villages and built-up areas. All Checkpoints are being manned by efficient marshals and sited away from dwellings to minimise potential problems. All gates across the roads that are to be used will be opened and closed by officials, to ensure the safety to stock on the land.

A representative of the organising Club will be visiting all isolated farmhouses or dwellings that are close to the route to ensure that residents are aware of the plans and to assure them that every effort will be made to protect their peace of mind. Finally competitors will all be notified that any undue nuisance or noise created by them during the event will mean their instant disqualification from the event. We know that many people along the route will be taking an interest in our passage and a great number will be watching the cars go by at several points.

The first competing car should be passing near to your property from .... to .... at .... and the last one at .... There may be a few minutes difference in these times either way, but they should not be far off.

May we thank you for your kind indulgence, and suggest that if you have any point or matter that you would like to raise, you contact us, and we will endeavour to clarify it for you.

We are very fond of our sport, and do not want damage caused to its name for lack of a little care in preparation.

You may be interested in watching this event yourself, if so please let me know and I will arrange for you to receive a free copy of the entry list.

SIGNED.... S. Lawrenson
(Chief PR Officer)

Public Relations work is absolutely essential if a road rally is to cause no problems. This is the sort of letter which must be delivered to EVERY householder on the route.

Clear reliable time pieces should be used by all marshals and these marshals must be quite clear about their role in the event. They must be familiar with all the time cards which they will have to sign and they must use a consistent method of handling cars. It is no good stage marshals counting some cars down from ten to one,

then merely shouting the last three seconds to another car. There must always be an adequate number of marshals at each control and there must be a visual signal at 'go'.

Marshalling is an important part of rallying and we have already advocated that everyone should have a crack at the job, at least once in their life. Marshals control the progress of an event and, be it a road or stage rally, their efficiency can have a tremendous bearing on the success of a rally. Organisers should give as much information as possible to marshals. Such information should tell them about the event, their responsibilities and details of competitors. It must clearly define responsibilities – a Stage Finish marshal and a Car Park marshal are totally different beings.

Marshalling can be great fun but just occasionally marshals gain something of a power complex and though marshals are generally the much loved, unsung heroes of rallying there are one or two who do little to endear their club to competitors.

We advocated in an earlier chapter that competitors should be nice to marshals; we suggest that this ought to be reciprocated.

Marshals must be absolutely reliable and turn up at briefings and of course control points well in advance of their due times. They should be properly dressed for the occasion and should take plenty of spare clothing as well as umbrellas, spare torches, paper, maps, food and refreshments and anything else that makes the job more comfortable. Marshalling is an interesting job and can be very satisfying as well.

While on the subject of marshals we should at this point mention the paperwork which will have to be issued to them. The Chief Marshal will have the responsibility of having these printed and mailed but will, of course, work under the close eye of the Clerk of the Course for many is the marshal who has found himself experiencing a particularly quiet night as a result of being sent the wrong map reference for a control!

Ideally, each marshal should be posted a detailed diagram of his control and the direction of approach and departure of the

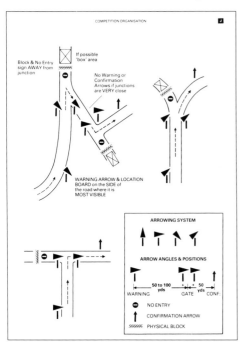

Block & No Entry sign AWAY from junction

If possible 'box' area

No Warning or Confirmation Arrows if junctions are VERY close

WARNING ARROW & LOCATION BOARD on the SIDE of the road where it is MOST VISIBLE

ARROWING SYSTEM

ARROW ANGLES & POSITIONS

WARNING — 50 to 100 yds — GATE — 50 yds — CONF.

- NO ENTRY

CONFIRMATION ARROW

SSSSS PHYSICAL BLOCK

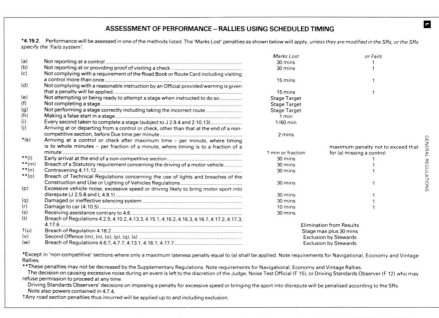

*4.19.2. Performance will be assessed in one of the methods listed. The 'Marks Lost' penalties as shown below will apply, *unless they are modified in the SRs, or the SRs specify the 'Fails system'.*

		Marks Lost	or Fails
(a)	Not reporting at a control	30 mins	1
(b)	Not reporting at or providing proof of visiting a check	30 mins	1
(c)	Not complying with a requirement of the Road Book or Route Card including visiting a control more than once	15 mins	1
(d)	Not complying with a reasonable instruction by an Official provided warning is given that a penalty will be applied	15 mins	1
(e)	Not attempting or being ready to attempt a stage when instructed to do so	Stage Target	
(f)	Not completing a stage	Stage Target	
(g)	Not performing a stage correctly including taking the incorrect route	Stage Target	
(h)	Making a false start in a stage	1 min	
(i)	Every second taken to complete a stage (subject to J 2.9.4 and 2.10.13)	1/60 min	
(j)	Arriving at or departing from a control or check, other than that at the end of a non-competitive section, before Due time per minute	2 mins	
*(k)	Arriving at a control or check after maximum time – per minute, where timing is to whole minutes – per fraction of a minute, where timing is to a fraction of a minute	1 min or fraction	maximum penalty not to exceed that for (a) missing a control
**(l)	Early arrival at the end of a non-competitive section	30 mins	1
**(m)	Breach of a Statutory requirement concerning the driving of a motor vehicle	30 mins	1
**(n)	Contravening 4.11.12	30 mins	1
**(o)	Breach of Technical Regulations concerning the use of lights and breaches of the Construction and Use or Lighting of Vehicles Regulations	30 mins	1
(p)	Excessive vehicle noise, excessive speed or driving likely to bring motor sport into disrepute (J 2.5.8 and L 4.8.1)	30 mins	1
(q)	Damaged or ineffective silencing system	30 mins	1
(r)	Damage to car (4.10.5)	10 mins	1
(s)	Receiving assistance contrary to 4.6	30 mins	
(t)	Breach of Regulations 4.2.9, 4.10.2, 4.13.3, 4.15.1, 4.16.2, 4.16.3, 4.16.7, 4.17.2, 4.17.3, 4.17.6	Elimination from Results	
†(u)	Breach of Regulation 4.18.2	Stage max plus 30 mins	
(v)	Second Offence (m), (n), (o), (p), (q), (s)	Exclusion by Stewards	
(w)	Breach of Regulations 4.6.7, 4.7.7, 4.13.1, 4.16.1, 4.17.7	Exclusion by Stewards	

*Except in 'non-competitive' sections where only a maximum lateness penalty equal to (a) shall be applied. Note requirements for Navigational, Economy and Vintage Rallies.

**These penalties may not be decreased by the Supplementary Regulations. Note requirements for Navigational, Economy and Vintage Rallies.
The decision on causing excessive noise during an event is left to the discretion of the Judge, Noise Test Official (F 15), or Driving Standards Observer (F 12) who may refuse permission to proceed at any time.
Driving Standards Observers' decisions on imposing a penalty for excessive speed or bringing the sport into disrepute will be penalised according to the SRs.
Note also powers contained in 4.7.4.

†Any road section penalties thus incurred will be applied up to and including exclusion.

The standard system of arrowing stages is shown in the RACMSA 'Blue Book', as is the standard penalty system.

نهاية مرحلة خاصّة – ٤ مراقبين
FINISH OF SPECIAL STAGE – 4 MARSHALS

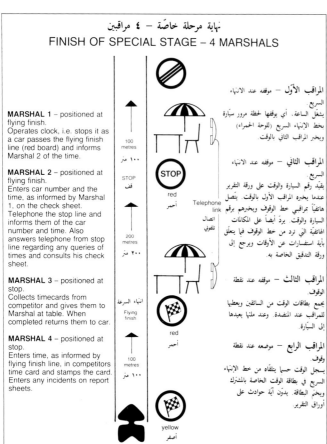

MARSHAL 1 – positioned at flying finish.
Operates clock, i.e. stops it as a car passes the flying finish line (red board) and informs Marshal 2 of the time.

MARSHAL 2 – positioned at flying finish.
Enters car number and the time, as informed by Marshal 1, on the check sheet. Telephone the stop line and informs them of the car number and time. Also answers telephone from stop line regarding any queries of times and consults his check sheet.

MARSHAL 3 – positioned at stop.
Collects timecards from competitor and gives them to Marshal at table. When completed returns them to car.

MARSHAL 4 – positioned at stop.
Enters time, as informed by flying finish line, in competitors time card and stamps the card. Enters any incidents on report sheets.

100 metres · ١٠٠ متر

STOP · قف · red · أحمر

Telephone link · اتصال تلفوني

200 metres · ٢٠٠ متر

انتهاء السرعة
Flying finish · red · أحمر

100 metres · ١٠٠ متر

yellow · أصفر

المراقب الأوّل – موقفه عند الانتهاء السريع.
يشغل الساعة. أي يوقفها لحظة مرور سيّارة خط الانتهاء السريع (للوحة الحمراء) ويخبر المراقب الثاني بالوقت.

المراقب الثاني – موقفه عند الانتهاء السريع.
يقيّد رقم السيارة والوقت على ورقة التقرير. يتصل هاتفياً بمراقبي خط الوقوف ويخبرهم برقم السيارة والوقت. يرد أيضاً على المكالمات الهاتفية التي ترد من خط الوقوف فإما يعلّى بأية استفسارات عن الأوقات ويرجع إلى ورقة التدقيق الخاصة به.

المراقب الثالث – موقفه عند نقطة الوقوف.
يجمع طاقات الوقت من السابقين ويعطيها للمراقب عند المنضدة. وعند ملئها يعيدها إلى السيّارة.

المراقب الرابع – موضعه عند نقطة وقوف.
يسجل الوقت حسبما يتلقّاه من خط الانتهاء السريع في بطاقة الوقت الخاصة بالمشترك ويختم الطاقة. يدوّن أية حوادث على أوراق التقرير.

Marshals' instructions must be explicit. These are from a Middle East event. Rallying is still relatively new to that part of the world.

Spectator Safety

Don't

- Stand on the track
- Stand below the level of the track
- Stand in front of arrows or signs
- Stand in Prohibited Areas
- Stand or sit on or near log piles walls or fences
- Sit close to the edge of the track
- Block escape routes
- Be distracted
- Play games with your safety or that of the drivers
- Remove Stage signs or arrows
- Be the one to stop the Stage

Study the diagrams - the shaded areas are 'No - Go'
Being there could cause delays or the cancellation of the Stage

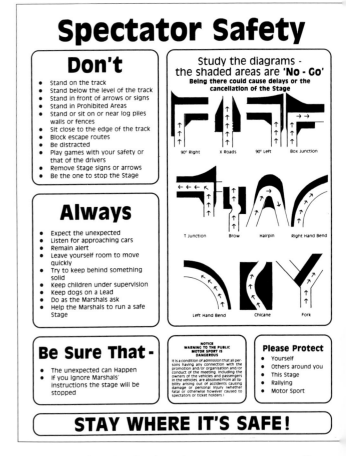

90° Right · X Roads · 90° Left · Box Junction

T Junction · Brow · Hairpin · Right Hand Bend

Left Hand Bend · Chicane · Fork

Always

- Expect the unexpected
- Listen for approaching cars
- Remain alert
- Leave yourself room to move quickly
- Try to keep behind something solid
- Keep children under supervision
- Keep dogs on a Lead
- Do as the Marshals ask
- Help the Marshals to run a safe Stage

Be Sure That -

- The unexpected can Happen
- If you ignore Marshals' instructions the stage will be stopped

NOTICE WARNING TO THE PUBLIC MOTOR SPORT IS DANGEROUS
It is a condition of admission that all persons having any connection with the promotion and/or organisation and/or conduct of the meeting, including the owners of the vehicles and passengers in the vehicles, are absolved from all liability arising out of accidents causing damage or personal injury (whether fatal or otherwise however caused) to spectators or ticket holders.

Please Protect

- Yourself
- Others around you
- This Stage
- Rallying
- Motor Sport

STAY WHERE IT'S SAFE!

Spectator safety is of prime importance to any rally organiser. The 'Blue Book' gives advice on the messages which must be put over to spectators.

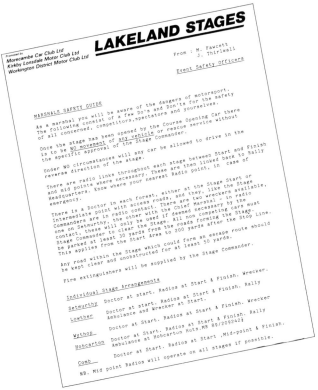

On a special stage event the marshals' instructions are strongly concerned with safety.

rally cars. Some organisers plot the route onto an O.S. map then cut it up into approximately 4 km squares, each featuring a control. These are then pasted onto the marshals' instructions.

The instructions for each control will detail the time due of the first car (in B.B.C. time, to avoid any confusion) and the time of opening the control (usually 30 minutes before the first car is due). The time of closing for the stage is also notified (generally 30 minutes after the time of arrival of the last expected car).

A marshal's check sheet should be sent out with the instructions – this may be incorporated in the instructions, to save printing costs. The sheet will feature a number of ruled lines – one for each car in the rally. The marshals will be required to mark in the time each car visits the control; this document can prove vital if proof of passage of a rally car is required at the finish. Naturally, the sheets should be handed in at the results headquarters.

The starting point of a rally is important if things are to go well. The most used rally start areas are garages or large petrol stations, although more important events may start from city squares, promenades or even from the town hall steps. Whatever starting facilities are chosen make sure that everything is clear and straightforward for competitors and spectators alike. Obviously it is important to have petrol available near to the start and it is usually not difficult to find a garage which will open specially to offer starting facilities in exchange for the petrol sales. There must be enough room for signing-on and adequate toilet facilities should be available.

How much you dress up the start of your rally depends upon the nature of the event and possibly what sponsorship you have, but an informed commentator and P.A. system is always a good thing. Even a few bits of well positioned bunting and a banner or two can add a sense of occasion!

Half-way stops and petrol halts are most important. The rally should be timed to give competitors adequate time for re-fuelling. When selecting a garage for a petrol halt, make sure that they know what they are in for and that they have adequate staff as well as adequate change and all the necessary facilities. Remember, too, that service cars and spectators will probably wish to fill up, so the petrol pump attendant should not be surprised if his two-pump/wooden shack emporium takes on the appearance of a motorway service station for a while.

In the case of an all-night rally, organisers should send someone to petrol halts well in advance of the rally – one important event collapsed at 3 a.m. when a garage owner forgot to open up!

Again, after an all-night rally the hotel or restaurant selected for the finish must have adequate catering and washing facilities and good car-parking space. Motorway service areas are often used although these can be a little impersonal and the rally prizegiving can lose something of its glamour if held in the corridor between the Transport Cafe and the "Gents".

In the case of bigger rallies where competitors and officials will be staying the night, it is important to have a good working relationship with hotels selected as starting or finishing points. Many hotel groups now actively encourage rallies to start and finish at their premises.

When the rally has disappeared, all signs of it should have similarly vanished. The sport of rallying will not endear itself to the general public if it leaves a string of empty oil-cans in its wake.

A good rally can be ruined if results take a long time to appear so it is important that a smooth system is developed to produce results and to keep competitors furnished with information about their performance as the event progresses. Most rallies use telephone links between their headquarters and personnel in the field. It is sensible to put up lists of penalties at frequent intervals at the rally finish to keep people interested until the full results are posted. Printed sets of results should be mailed to all competitors as soon as possbile after the event and it is a courtesy to send them to all the marshals and other interested parties too.

Rally organisers are a masochistic breed but, on the whole, a very friendly lot. If you are a beginner and really fancy organising an event, no matter how small, make contact with an established rally organiser in your locality. He will be very happy to put you on the right lines. Rally organisation is an exacting and responsible job as the smallest mistake can have serious repercussions.

As with so many other aspects of rallying, the key message is: pay attention to detail. This applies to safety as much as to the rest of a rally.

Motor sport can be dangerous and whether you are involved in rallying as a driver, marshal or spectator, you are more likely to come across an accident than the average motorist, so it makes sense to know a little about first aid. The following points are not intended to be exhaustive – just a brief guide to what to do at an accident.

● *Protect the scene of the accident by sending someone up the road to slow or stop following cars. If you get hurt you won't be able to help anyone.*

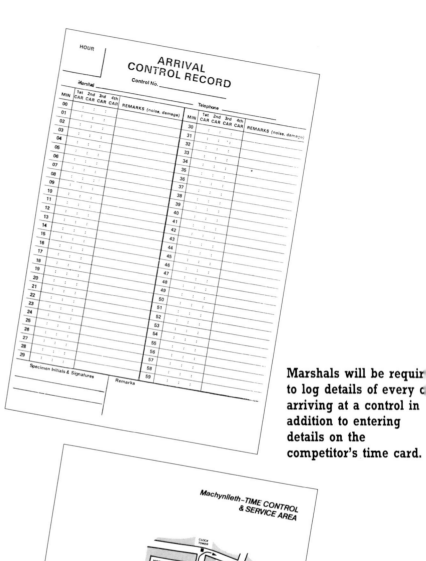

Marshals will be requir to log details of every c arriving at a control in addition to entering details on the competitor's time card.

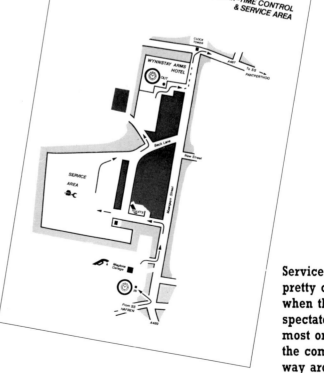

Service areas can becom pretty confusing places when thousands of spectators turn up so most organisers will he the competitor find his way around.

- *Switch off ignitions and stop people smoking – obvious, of course, but people with frayed nerves may light up.*

- *Check the breathing of any casualties not able to speak. If someone is NOT breathing, tilt their head back, pinch their nose shut and blow air into their lungs – their chest should rise. Remove your mouth from the casualty's mouth, let air out; repeat every five seconds until breathing restarts. (This is mouth-to-mouth resuscitation and is one of the most important things to learn; try to see a practical demonstration sometime – it's not difficult.)*

- *If someone is bleeding badly, press on the bleeding area firmly with your fingers, thumb and hand; if help is available, replace with dry dressing and a firm bandage. Ensure that bleeding stops – if not, revert to hand pressure.*

- *Do not remove a casualty from a car unless there is a real danger, eg fire*

or drowning, because they may have a fractured spine. Wait for skilled help.

- *Unconscious casualties outside a vehicle should be placed in the "3/4 prone position", i.e. almost face down. Ensure that they are breathing easily –if not, apply mouth to mouth resuscitation; DO NOT LEAVE until they regain consciousness.*

- *Send someone to get skilled help – ambulance, rescue vehicle, etc.*

- *Remember that things which fall off a rally car may be very HOT. Kick broken exhausts out of the way, don't pick them up.*

- *Try not to panic. It may not be easy but if you can keep calm while everyone else is flapping about you may save someone's life.*

Perhaps it's not a bad idea for organisers to print advice along the above lines on the back of one of their instruction sheets to rally officials. ◼

THE CLASSIC RALLIES

There are many good rallies for the young enthusiast to aim for during his career but only a few have that magical mixture of a tough route, good organisation, some tradition and, above all, that intangible ingredient X which makes them classics. In the authors' opinions, three stand above the rest:

The Monte Carlo Rally

The only event with more than one starting point, it is far and away the best known rally – in market research exercises it is often the *only* rally identified by the general public. Mind you, this may be diluted in due course by the *Paris-Dakar*, an amazing 'raid' event, although perhaps more for adventurers than 'conventional' rally drivers.

Occasional organisational lapses over the years may have tarnished the legend slightly among competitors but the Monte itself still gets large entries, with a high proportion of private owners, battling it out over some glorious special stages.

All the stages are on surfaced roads, closed to the public for the rally but all open for practising beforehand.

The final stage of the Monte can be one of the most dramatic in rallying – keep an eye open in rally films for shots taken at the top of the classic Turini. Magic! Occasionally, hooligan spectators spread snow on unexpected corners which is less than entertaining.

Don't be put off by the works teams and their 1000 or so tyres per car; beg, borrow or steal some old studded tyres, mortgage the house, sell the hi-fi and have a go at it; you will be able to dine out on it for months.

There are not so many Beautiful People about on the rally as at the Grand Prix but Monte in January can still be very pleasant.

The Lombard R.A.C. Rally

As your 'home' classic this is certainly one you should work towards in your development as a rally driver.

Spectator interest has to be seen to be believed. In fact, the enthusiasm causes problems because stages sometimes have to be cancelled because of crowd congestion.

Despite a high entry fee (because of forestry charges) it is still a 'must' in your competition career. If you want to get noticed by the works teams, grit your teeth and try to lead the rally by the end of the first day. Better still, try to lead it by the end of the last day!

The Safari

Some of the mystery has filtered away now that several Europeans have won the Safari but it still remains a tremendous challenge against time and the elements. One of the few rallies not divided into 'stages'. It is one stage from start to finish – usually at an average of over 60 mph! Then remember that it is either very, very, wet or very, very, muddy and you see why it is for men, not boys.

The Safari takes place entirely in Kenya (at Easter) and, because of the travel costs, is well nigh prohibitively expensive for

No event offers more 'atmosphere' than the Monte Carlo Rally. This Renault slithers past a well patronised watering-hole!

The Lombard R.A.C. Rally is still regarded by many drivers as the toughest of them all. The forests provide a variety of surfaces and obstacles.

Now you know why they're called 'Flying Finns'! This particular one is Markku Alén on the 1000 Lakes Rally - the fastest rally in the world.

European private owners (which is one reason why it does not have a huge entry). Mind you, if you can get there somehow you needn't be deterred by the calibre of the entry which falls off badly after the first dozen or so cars.

Be prepared for Safari fever - in other words, nerves - which sometimes puts even the most experienced drivers on edge. There is no known antidote.

The battles between the top teams over service arrangements are almost as entertaining as the rally - but don't blame them for laying on lavish plans when every service point is practically a pit stop: if someone passes you while you are at a service point you may have to follow in their dust for miles.

Long may the Safari survive. It probably will - as long as it attracts world interest as

The Acropolis is the roughest, rockiest rally in Europe.

The Manx International provides fast tarmac stages – unusual in Britain.

it does at present (including extensive coverage on Japanese TV).

Incidentally, although this book isn't intended to be a travel guide, Kenya is worth a visit just for the wildlife.

So those are our three classics. Two others worth considering:

The 1000 Lakes Rally

This Finnish event is well known mainly because of the outstanding reputation of Finnish rally drivers, and is often the first time future 'stars' become noticed. The winners have usually covered colossal practice miles, although pressure from residents on the rally route has led to strict limits on recce speeds being imposed – a foretaste of what is likely to apply everywhere.

If you think of Finns as wild men, be prepared for a shock when you see them on the road sections – they are meticulous in obeying speed limits because there are heavy rally penalties for breaking the law; the police have been known to put rally stickers on otherwise plain cars in order to catch people speeding!

You may see marks made on roads on

the stages – these are where spectators have wagered who will 'yump' the furthest among their heroes. There are regularly 10,000 paying spectators on stages – very well controlled by marshals with Alsatian dogs.

The Acropolis

A great stage event over rough roads and what look like goat tracks. A qualifying event for six national (as well as the world) championships and usually a big entry.

Very tough, very fast, very demanding but . . . don't shy away. Greece is glorious at the time of the year and it is an ideal rally to combine with a holiday: take your car down on a trailer because you stand a fair chance of breaking down.

Some others

Much less expensive than the above is the 24 Hours of Ypres Rally in Belgium. With easy to recce stages this is an ideal event for someone tackling a foreign rally for the first time. There are other Belgian and Dutch events which are well worth a thought.

Even nearer home, the Welsh and Scottish have a lot of attraction, both being excellent practise for the Lombard R.A.C. Rally. The Scottish is rough and you may get through a lot of tyres but it is a super event through splendid country and with a fine social side.

The Welsh is one of the cheapest of the home classics and a 'must' on your way to tackling the Lombard R.A.C.

The Manx also provides a relatively cheap event (and all costs are 'relative' in the expensive world of motorsport) with high speed tarmac stages where you can practise pace-notes.

If Easter in Ireland is your scene then the Circuit of Ireland will be high on your list. But don't be lulled by the social side – it is a tough, demanding rally. Tarmac stages on closed roads add to the joy. Limited practising is allowed although obviously the classic stages get well known, being used year after year.

Some would argue that the Swedish Rally is better than the 1000 Lakes. Certainly it is

different, being the only World Championship event held entirely on snow and ice. Regulations on studded tyres might mean you need special ones just for the one event, and it is a lot colder in Sweden in winter than in Finland in August!

Very expensive and a long way away but with a character all of its own is the Tour de Corse. Thousands and thousands of corners with sheer drops on many of them mean it is not for the faint-hearted although, curiously, if you've done Welsh road rallies you won't feel totally at sea in Corsica. One of life's more enriching experiences!

Finally, keep an eye open for the "odd balls" – rallies run in weird and wonderful places for the strangest reasons. Show interest and present a good case and you could end up getting financial support from organisers who are working closely with tourist boards and airlines.

If you find the loot to tackle a programme of major events, you may get interested in one of the championships:

World Rally Championship for Makes and Drivers

A very expensive series to do and few manufacturers tackle all the rounds in this Championship. There tends to be a battle between the manufacturers who want a limited number of qualifying events (ideally eight), and the organisers who – understandably – all want 'their' event in the World Championship. Until this is resolved and all the key manufacturers do all the qualifying events, it will be difficult for rallying to have the same general public appeal as, say, Formula One, where all cars and drivers do all the qualifying rounds.

The series includes a World Rally *Drivers* championship – because (hard though it may be for manufacturers to accept) people are interested in people.

Finally there is a European Rally Championship with lots of qualifying events – generally shorter than the World Championship ones. But although championships may be useful to tie the sport together, our advice would be to simply do the rallies which

Timo Salonen in his element on the Snowy Swedish Rally

The Tour de Corse is fast and furious . . . and the crowds love it!

interest either you or your sponsor (if you have one). If you need further convincing, stop the next one hundred people you see and ask them who is the current European Rally Champion (or World Champion for that matter). Very few will know. ■

TEAMS & SERVICE CREWS

The Team

Like much to do with rallying, organisation is the key to a successful rally team. All parts of the team must work efficiently and nothing must be left to chance. When organising a rally team the most unexpected must always be expected; that may sound 'double Dutch' but a professional team will try to plan for every contingency before it actually happens. The Team manager of a professional team will make sure that his service cars carry the most obscure spare parts and everything will have been checked fully and nothing left to chance.

Even then, some things are totally unforeseeable. Many years ago Timo Makinen made a call for snow tyres for a Scottish Rally. Yes, the sunny Scottish Rally! It was quite unthinkable that it would snow in Scotland in June and Dunlops thought Ford's Team Manager had taken leave of his senses when snow tyres were ordered. You've guessed – it snowed in the Highlands and covered several stages. Like many Finns, Makinen had a fixation about snow accoutrements and once had snow chains flown out to Kenya to see if they'd work in red murrum mud! But enough of memory lane . . .

Here we give examples of some of the things that a professional team might organise when competing on a typical international event. On some rallies like the Safari or Monte Carlo there might be special problems needing a great deal of attention; on other events the problems might be simpler. For instance, there might be no tyre choices or no overseas travel to worry about – two of the most time-consuming projects.

If a team is competing in an overseas event all travel movements must be planned in detail. Boat and air tickets should be booked in good time, especially at peak holiday times, and a travel itinerary be produced.

Plenty of time must be allowed for personnel to get to the start of a rally, particularly mechanics and service cars. Mechanics should be given time to check over cars before the start and drivers time to test them.

Most teams produce a booklet giving instructions to service crews, ranging from general notes about the positions of service boards and mobile radio to detailed rally car arrival times at service points. Instructions for drivers and navigators will also be included and will cover topics as varied as hotel reservations, emergency telephone numbers and even notes on known sections of route. A team 'Bible' can run to over 150 pages for a complicated international event.

Long before an event, an organised team will have numerous meetings where drivers and mechanics compare notes, discuss the rally and its mechanical requirements and make plans in detail. These planning meetings between team managers, drivers, navigators and mechanics always pay dividends.

A team should always hold a briefing meeting before the start at which details of each service point are discussed fully so

LANGUAGE	HELP	WE NEED	A DOCTOR / AN AMBULANCE	A RESCUE VEHICLE / A FIRE EXTINGUISHER	CALL THE POLICE	I HAVE HURT MY	HEAD / CHEST	STOMACH / BACK	LEG / ARM	HAND / FOOT	DON'T MOVE ME / MY FRIEND
English	HELP	WE NEED	A DOCTOR / AN AMBULANCE	A RESCUE VEHICLE / A FIRE EXTINGUISHER	CALL THE POLICE	I HAVE HURT MY	HEAD / CHEST	STOMACH / BACK	LEG / ARM	HAND / FOOT	DON'T MOVE ME / MY FRIEND
Finnish	APUA	TARVITSEMME	LAAKARIN AMBULANSSIN	PELASTUSAUTON TULENSAMMUTTIMEN	KUTSUKAA POLISI	OLEN LOUKANNUT	PAAN / RINNAN	VATSAN / SELAN	VALAN / KASVARREN	KADEN / JALKATERAN	ALKAA LIIKUTTAKO MUA / YSTAVAM
Norwegian	HJELP	VI TRENGER	EN DOKTOR / EN AMBULANSE	BERGNINGSBIL / EN BRANNSLUKKER	RING TIL POLITIET	JEG HAR SKADET MITT	HODE / BRYST	MAGE / RYGG	BEIN / ARM	HAND / FOT	IKKE BEVEG MEG / MIN VENN
French	AU SECOURS	IL NOUS FAUT	UN MEDICIN / UNE AMBULANCE	VEHICULE DE DEPANNAGE / EXTINCTEUR	APPELEZ LA POLICE	JE ME SUIS FAIT MAL	A LA TETE / A LA POITRINE	AU VENTRE / AU DOS	A LA JAMBE / AU BRAS	A LA MAIN / AU PIED	NE LE TOUCHEZ PAS /
Swedish	HJALP	VI BEHOVER	EN LAKARE / EN AMBULANS	EN BARGNINGSBIL / EN BRANDSLAKARE	TILLKALLA POLIS	JAG HAR SKADAT MITT	HVVUD / BROST	MAGE / RYGG	BEN / ARM	HAND / FOT	FLYTTA INTE MEJ / MIN VAN
Italian	AUTO	ABBIAMO BESOGNO DI	UN MEDICO / UN AMBULANZA	UN MESSO DI SECORSO / UNESTINTORE	CHIAMATE LA POLIZIA	SONO FERITO AL'	LA TESTA / LA TORACE	LO STOMACO / LA SCHENA	LA GAMBA / LA BRACCIO	LA MANA / LA PIEDE	NON MUOVETE MI / MI AMICO
German	HILFE	ICH BRANCHE	EINE ARZT / EINEN KLINIK	EINEN KANKENWAGEN / EINEN FEUERLOSCHER	RUFEN SIE DIE POLIZEI	ICH HABE MICH VERLETZT AM	KOPF / BRUST	MAGEN / RUCKEN	BEIN / ARM	HAND / FUSS	BEWEGEN SIE NICHT MEIN FREUNDE
Spanish	AYUDA	NECESITAMOS	UN MEDICO / UNA AMBULICIA	UN AUTO DE SOCORRO / UN EXTINGUADOR	LLAME LA POLICIA	ME DUELE	LA CABEZA / EL PECHO	EL ESTOMAGO / LA ESPULDA	LA PIERNA / EL BRAZO	LA MANO / EL PIE	NO LO MUEVA
Turkish	YARDIM	ISTIYORUZ	DOKTOR / CANKURTARAN	KURTARICI / SONDURUCU LAZIM	POLISI ARAYIN	YARALI	BASIMDAN / GOGSUM	KARNIM / SIRTIM	BACAGIM / KOLUM	ELIM / AYAGIM	ONU KIMILDATMAYIN
Dutch	HELP	WE HEBBEN EEN NADIG	DOKTER / AMBULANCE	KRAANWAGEN / BRANDBLUSSER	BEL DE POLITIE	IK BEN GEWOND AAN MIJN	HOOFD / BORST	MAAG / RUG	BEEN / ARM	HAND / VOET	BEWEEG NIET MIJ / MIJN VRIEND
Portuguese	AJUDEM	ME NECESSITO	UM MEDICO / UMA AMBULICIA	UM REBOQUE / UM EXTINTOR	CHAME A POLICIA	MAGOEI/FERI A	CABECA / TORAZU	ESTOMAGO / COSTAS	PERNA / BRACO	MAO / PE	NAO (ME/MEY. AMIGO) TOQUEM

A Glossary of language translations is from an original idea by F.I. de Dombal MA, MD, FRCS, written by I.R.D.C. members worldwide for the I.R.D.C. the
Medical Officers Group (Yorkshire) and the World Organisation of Gastro-Enterology

The International Rally Drivers Club produce some excellent booklets to help people rallying abroad. This one shows useful phrases in eleven languages and could be useful for service crews as well as drivers.

There's intense pressure all the time in international rallying. Carlos Sainz explains his problems to assorted engineers and journalists.

team members may be paying for everything out of their own pockets. Nevertheless, without being dictatorial, the person whose job it is to handle the team should try to follow the guidelines set by the professionals. The main thing is to keep everyone informed at all times. Let there be no secrets.

Service crews

Throughout this book we have referred to service crews and their importance cannot be underestimated. Although their presence is not necessarily welcome, and almost certainly forbidden on road rallies, there is no doubt that service crews are a necessary part of stage rallying. As speeds of rally cars increase, as stages become rougher and as rallies become longer the more important become the service crews.

There may be a vast difference between the professional works service crew and the amateur, but by describing some of the methods of the former, we hope that amateurs might benefit. To works service crews the rally is a job of work for which they are paid and whilst they are totally dedicated to their job and to the sport, they cannot be expected to do anything 'purely for love of it'. In other words, they will be paid at the appropriate rate for the job and

that everyone is familiar with his own role on the event. A well-organised team will arrange tickets for post-rally functions and will even give advice on dress before and after the event. For instance, team ties, sweaters or blazers help to give a team a tidy, professional image and should be supplied to all personnel if budgets will run to them.

Running a rally team is just like running any other sports team, be it professional or amateur. Everything must knit together and it is the responsibility of the Team Manager or his deputy to see that harmony abounds.

If you are running your own small team – maybe made up of club members – it will be a little more difficult to play the heavy hand as a Team Manager for, after all, the

Service schedules should be clear and easily understood. For the Lombard RAC Rally Lancia issue a detailed marked copy of the Ordnance Survey map accompanied by instructions in English and Italian.

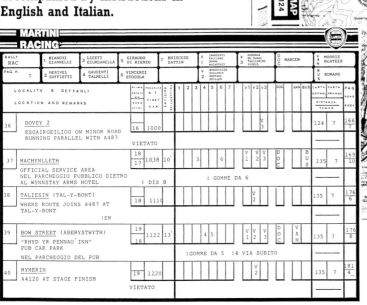

should be provided with first class equipment.

A good service crew will consist of two or three mechanics in an estate car or van. They should all be capable of all types of mechanical work, although one or other may have special knowledge of some particular subject, for example: electrics or engines. They will have every conceivable spare part on board although obviously nothing unnecessary will be carried as the weight of the service vehicle is important.

It obviously helps if service crew personnel are competent drivers and at least one member of the crew should be competent at map reading, with the ability to plot references, interpret time schedules and generally keep the service car on the right route.

To see any real expert doing his job to the best of his ability is a joy, and to see a rally mechanic working with precision at high speed under difficult conditions (such as in sub-zero temperatures or in mud and rain) is as exciting as watching a star driver in full cry: crowds at service points endorse this.

Like all professionals, good rally me-

chanics will take certain precautions when preparing a car and may alter brackets and mounting points to facilitate removal and replacement of parts when valuable seconds count (taking care not to break homologation rules, of course). They even

Dave Metcalfe enjoys a lengthy service stop on the Circuit of Ireland.

long way from home! New ealander 'Possum' Bourne's ubaru takes routine service.

ll hands on deck for rwin Weber's VW.

make special tools which can get into awkward spots and so save further vital seconds.

Many people think that the life of an international works rally mechanic is one of glamorous jet-setting and mingling with the famous. True, these things do come into the mechanic's life but 90% of his life is pure, solid, honest-to-goodness hard work. He probably enjoys travelling and seeing new places but it is remarkable how quickly mechanics become accustomed to the glamorous surroundings to which their work takes them. Some might think that they are rather blasé about the whole thing. It won't be uncommon to hear two rally mechanics sitting beneath the tailgate of their service car in a remote African village

discussing the latest doings of Manchester United or Nottingham Forest, oblivious of their exotic location!

Service crews must be equipped with the right clothing, whatever climate they are working in. They should always carry at least two pairs of overalls each (one for working in dirty conditions and the other for use at scrutineering and other times when they are not expecting to become covered with mud). They should have good strong boots (some prefer sporting shoes for greater agility), warm underwear and extra sets of waterproof gear. A warm, fur-lined 'Parka' is a good thing to have as well. Don't expect a service mechanic to wear a rally jacket for work and manage to keep it clean; he'll have to be equipped with more than one rally jacket. As we have said elsewhere, oily rally jackets in hotel bars do not present a good team image.

Preparation of the service car or van is almost as important as the preparation of the rally car. First and foremost, it is wise to build a solid grille between the driver's compartment and the rear area, as accidents have happened as a result of jacks, welding bottles or halfshafts flying about inside the vehicle. Furthermore, everything which is heavy should be strapped down. A roof rack may be necessary to carry extra wheels and bigger

A typical road-side service point on a British international rally. Service crews should make sure they have due regard for the countryside and other road users. Wherever possible organisers will site service areas off the public road.

items. Inside the vehicle there should be plenty of small drawers for every conceivable size of nut, bolt and washer. Drawers and compartments should be labelled and things stored in a logical way.

There should be plenty of light inside the rear of the service vehicle and several spare torches as well as a powerful inspection light which should have a lead long enough to reach right round the car. Many teams have bright floodlights to illuminate the service area

When a works service crew arrives at its predetermined spot (well ahead of its first potential customer) it will park off the public highway, on level ground if possible. It is common for numerous service cars to cluster together in lay-bys or service areas and, particularly if crews will not be certain where the mechanics will be, it will be helpful to have a good luminous or even illuminated service board carrying the team badge or some simple message or code: long-winded messages are not necessary. A private team's service crew once inadvertently left their board behind after leaving a service point in a Welsh village. The board was, in fact, a modified

Service vehicles can cause more trouble than rally cars, so very often the organisers will give details of service areas and the routes to be taken. These instructions were issued on the Gwynedd Rally.

Question! How many mechanics can fit into one Audi?

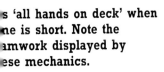

s 'all hands on deck' when
ne is short. Note the
amwork displayed by
ese mechanics.

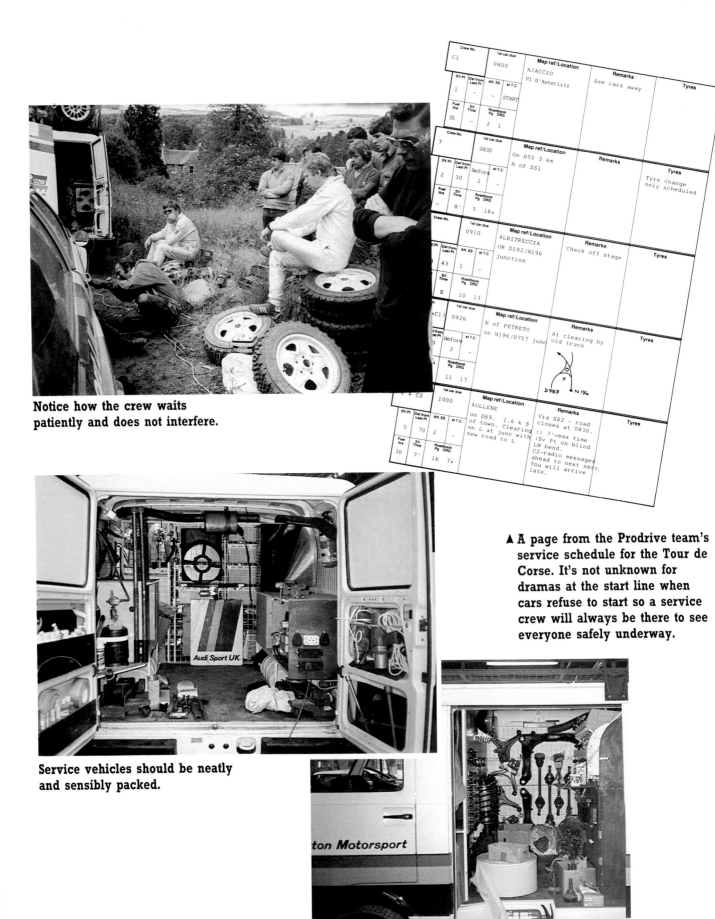

Notice how the crew waits
patiently and does not interfere.

Service vehicles should be neatly
and sensibly packed.

Crew No.	1st car due	Map ref/Location	Remarks	Tyres
C1	0800	AJACCIO Pl d'Auterlitz	See cars away	
SV.Pt 1	Dist from Last Pt –	Aft. SS – / at T.C. START		
Fuel ltrs 35	SV. Time –	Roadbook Pg 2 / DRG 1		

Crew No.	1st car due	Map ref/Location	Remarks	Tyres
7	0830	On D55 3 km N of SS1		Tyre change only scheduled
SV.Pt 2	Dist from Last Pt 30	Aft. SS Before / at T.C. –		
Fuel ltrs –	SV. Time 8'	Roadbook Pg 5 / DRG 18+		

Crew No.	1st car due	Map ref/Location	Remarks	Tyres
8	0910	ALBITRECCIA OR D102/N196 junction	Check off stage	
SV.Pt	Dist from Last Pt 43	Aft. SS 1 / at T.C. –		
SV. Time E		Roadbook Pg 10 / DRG 13		

Crew No.	1st car due	Map ref/Location	Remarks	Tyres
(+C1)	0926	N of PETRETO on N196/D757 junc	At clearing by old truck	
Dist from Last Pt	Before / at T.C. 2			
Roadbook Pg 11 / DRG 17		D757 N196		

Crew No.	1st car due	Map ref/Location	Remarks	Tyres
+ C2	1000	AULLENE on D69. 1.6 k S of town. Clearing on L at junc with new road to L	Via SS2 – road closes at 0830. !! 7'=max time !Sv pt on blind LH bend. C2-radio messages ahead to next serv. You will arrive late.	
SV.Pt 5	Dist from Last Pt 70	Aft. SS 2 / at T.C. –		
Fuel ltrs 30	SV. Time 7'	Roadbook Pg 16 / DRG 7+		

▲ A page from the Prodrive team's
service schedule for the Tour de
Corse. It's not unknown for
dramas at the start line when
cars refuse to start so a service
crew will always be there to see
everyone safely underway.

o, not a nasty accident. his is how they used to ork on Mini-Coopers in the ixties!

Heavy items in a service car must be well strapped down to stop them flying into mechanics in an accident.

pilots approaching Heathrow Airport!

All professional teams use radios and these can be a boon to a service crew on any size of event; for example mechanics can guide a rally driver to them at a congested service point by describing exactly where they are. Ensure that radios are legal, licensed, tuned to the right wavelength and that the organisers have not banned their use for any reason. Also keep in mind others may be listening in if you have to discuss confidential or sensitive matters.

A service crew should keep the radio 'live' at all times in case there's an emergency call for assistance from their rally car. You'd be surprised how many times rally cars have minor mechanical 'panics' and scream for assistance. Very often on an event like the Lombard R.A.C., the Acropolis or the San Remo, an 'off-duty' service crew driving to their next service point will pick up the call and give help. They must be careful not to be late at their next service point, of course, thereby jeopardising the rest of the team.

On normal occasions, the co-driver will radio forward to a service crew and advise them of the car's approximate time of arrival, the jobs that need to be done and the amount of time available. The good mechanic will then lay out the appropriate tools, not unlike a surgeon preparing for an operation.

When organising service, always try to avoid breaking the rules. Service areas – or, more importantly, forbidden service areas – will be shown by the organisers. They are given for a reason, so obey them.

Most teams resort to unmarked supervision cars and there is now a tendency to employ 'chase' cars which virtually cover the rally route. When vital World Championship points are at stake, teams have been known to enter cars purely as support vehicles, the 'navigators' of these cars being mechanics. Where will it all end? Mind you, racing and rally cars used to carry 'riding mechanics' fifty years ago. Maybe we've come full circle! ■

racing pit signal kit with removable letters. It was with some chagrin that they discovered, on a return visit to the village, their beloved sign outside a tea shop with the letters re-arranged to advertise cream teas!

Many service crews favour lights on long poles as a method of identifying their location. Hopefully, these can be seen above the rest of the rabble but in reality there are often so many tall poles carrying flashing lights that the view for the approaching rally crews is like that for

Money Matters

Glorious sport though it may be, rallying has one major problem: it is *expensive,* far more than football or golf, for instance. Nevertheless, thousands of people do compete every year and obviously find the funds somewhere, somehow and the better they manage their financial affairs, the more enjoyable and successful their efforts are likely to be. This chapter considers the financial side in two parts: spending the money and finding it. It may appear that we've got the two in the wrong order. Not so. If you haven't worked out what funds you need, and when, then you've no business approaching a sponsor for support.

Spending the money

The first thing to spend money on is a few sheets of paper. Sit down somewhere quiet, forget all the alleged glamour and excitement of rallying and *plan.* If you think things through carefully you will be able to save yourself time, money and heartache; a lot of programmes founder half way through a season through lack of planning.

Among the things to consider when planning are:

● Where you want to go in rallying? Are you content to just have fun or do you want to become a superstar? This will affect what sort of events you should compete in and how long you should stay in one particular area.

● What free time you have. Will a busy rally programme get in the way of a career and, if so, will it be worth the sacrifice? Remember that there isn't too much demand for old, unsuccessful rally drivers.

● Your ability. Be ruthlessly realistic. If you've been to a rally school or done several events and shown no promise, stop dreaming.

● The events you enjoy doing most. If you don't need to consider stepping stones to stardom then you should aim to get the most fun for your money. As an example, you could tackle a Continental rally for the cost of a Lombard-RAC Rally, do just as well, get as much fun, damage your car less, and tell far more uncheckable tall stories afterwards.

● The money you have available and your chances of raising more from sponsors.

Having carefully considered what rally programme to do, based on your broad planning, it is worth jotting down an objective for your programme, e.g. 'do six events, finish in the top 20 on the first two, in the top 10 on three of the remaining four events and collect at least one class win during the year'. That may all sound more calculating than just going out on a Sunday morning to kick a football about for a pub team but you will be spending a lot more, isn't it therefore worth more planning?

The next step is to draw up a budget, equally ruthlessly and realistically. Include everything in your budget and we do mean everything. Assume something will go wrong and allow plenty for contingencies.

Among the costs you will need to include are:

● Car purchase cost. Or will you be able to hire or even borrow one? Remember that, with luck, a car will still be worth something at the end of the programme.

● Preparation costs. A lot will depend on your driving ability but, remember, power costs money and don't tune ahead of your skills – it's a waste of money and could be dangerous.

● Running costs. In other words, what you will need to keep the car operating during the season. Try to resist the temptation to buy spares which have fallen off lorries; the police have been known to be the next thing to come over the tail board.

● Tyres. These could be included under running costs but are worth showing as a separate item, if only to bring home to you the importance and cost of the blasted things.

● Travel, hotels, meals. These items on your budget will obviously depend very much on your programme; if you are doing local rallies your costs may be minimal. If you have a more ambitious programme but limited funds remember it is better to spend what funds you have on the car, not on five-star hotels.

● Fuel. Self-explanatory but don't forget to include support vehicles, if any.

● Entry fees, licences, insurance. Again self-explanatory but don't skimp on the latter. Cover yourself as well as the car, particularly as you have dependent relatives.

● Plus . . . well, plus anything else you can think of. You may need a trailer to transport your car; co-drivers will obviously need to budget for maps.

Add it all up; pick yourself up off the floor; add at least 10% for contingencies; add it all up again and then check your individual calculations. For instance, if the average entry fee for your chosen rallies is X and you are doing six events, have you listed 6X or just X by mistake?

Unless you are very wealthy (and if so, why did you borrow this book from a library instead of buying it?) it is almost certain that, however optimistic you are about sponsorship, the total figure will be too high for your resources. Far too high.

So re-think your programme. Will selecting different events help? Paradoxically, it could be cheaper to do one foreign event than two home-based ones, because some overseas organisers will offer help with travel as well as free hotels and entries. Above all, remember that it is better to do four events adequately financed than five or six on a shoestring.

If you are falling about at the idea of all this budgeting just for your proposed

Sponsorship can come from various quarters but stickers on the car are only part of the story.

programme of club rallies, well you are misguided – honestly. It really is worth spending a little time planning things.

Two final points on this sordid saga of the cash draining away: work out a rough cash flow chart, that is a sheet showing what state your finances are likely to be in at the end of each month and, finally, let your bank manager know what you are up to. He will not loan you money for a motor-sport programme without adequate security but he may tide you over the odd low points (say when you are waiting for a quarterly sponsor's cheque). If you are very lucky, or believe in fairies, your bank may even give you direct sponsorship support. But don't

bank on it.

All a bit grim isn't it? But don't despair, let's move on to:

Finding the money

If you are wealthy or have rich friends or married well, then this section may not be for you. But most people will be glad of help. It would be unwisely optimistic to budget for any prize money at this stage (and remember there is no secondhand market for engraved cups) but you may be able to get a little trade support, e.g. free oil; adjust your budget accordingly. For most people, however, the aim will be to find a more generous sponsor. But before you set off on your search for a sponsor, ask yourself two things:

1 Are you putting in all you can afford yourself? The authors often hear people moaning that they can't afford a decent rally programme. But the moaners are revealed to have expensive boats, motorbikes or whatever. If they are not prepared to bleed a little by selling such things why should sponsors help them?

2 What makes you think you deserve support from a sponsor? No-one would help you if you announced to a breathless world that you were taking up snooker. Why should they help you into rallying? This point is not included to depress you but to keep your feet on the ground and make you realise what a struggle it is likely to be to find a sponsor.

It is important to regard sponsorship as a fee for a service rendered, not a gift and, like any business relationship, sponsorship must be a two-way exchange. A driver must give value.

But how do you find sponsorship?

Well, even though you may be an amateur driver you should still try to be professional in your approach and this means being realistic. If you are a young, unknown driver there will be little point in approaching national companies – far better to look locally.

Prepare a letter or document (which must be typed and well laid out) spelling out your plans and set out what you can offer a sponsor. For instance:

● You, your car and your support team in the sponsor's livery. Different licence grades allow different levels of advertising on cars. Basically a driver/entrant's licence allows you to have the name of the entrant, driver and make of car in lettering approximately four inches high on each side of the car, plus a maximum of five decals on each side, each no bigger than the size of a shoe box lid.

Any further advertising requires an advertising permit from the RACMSA. This permit allows unlimited advertising subject to certain provisos and is available in three grades – Restricted (£65), National (£143) and International (£290). With these licences you can paint almost anything on the car provided it isn't obscene of course. Also you will have to fork out another £58 for an entrant's licence if you want your sponsor's name in the rally programme.

Encourage a sponsor to work with you to develop a proper colour scheme for the car. Don't however, get too carried away with clever colours and graphics without checking that they photograph well. After all, one of the objectives should be to get sponsors shown in black and white photographs in newspapers and magazines.

If possible, send a sketch of how a car could look in a potential sponsor's colours; maybe even send a decorated model car as an attention grabber.

● You and the car available for promotions, e.g., in showrooms, trade fairs, even at town fairs and carnivals.

● Opportunities for media coverage. This even applies to raw drivers. 'Company X sponsor young Anytown driver' as a press clipping may appeal to companies who want to show they are a caring part of the community.

● The chance for sponsors to entertain customers at rallies; this is less common than with circuit racing but opportunities do arise.

● An opportunity to enthuse sponsors' staff by giving them a 'team' to follow.

● Drives or rides in the car for sponsors' staff or customers. This is one of the most effective ways of giving sponsors value.

● Promotional opportunities with badges. T-shirts, stickers, etc., with the sponsor's name. As you get better known, even have give-away photographs of yourself with sponsor identification.

Rather than give an outline of your

Rallying can be a major marketing weapon for a manufacturer – particularly if the product is linked to the motoring market.

A good sponsor for an expensive sport!

Make sure the sponsors are given good exposure on rally regulations and all other printed matter. These show two different classes of event.

proposed budget, offer to meet sponsors to discuss your plans (and their possible involvement) in more detail. Make sure any documentation is well typed and sent to the right person; research the company you are approaching and address a letter to the decision maker by name. Follow the letter up with a telephone call in a week or so's time and, if you do get an interview, be realistic. If you are starting on a rally career, sponsors will not be impressed if the first item on your budget is a huge hospitality unit.

We don't want to depress you but if you follow all the above advice, do appreciate that a lot of other people will also be searching, and not just from motorsport. Determination is a key factor in the character of a star driver – you will need all of yours at this stage in finding a sponsor. Marketing managers get countless approaches from netball teams, young men and women golfers, snooker championships and so on; many of them will offer far better exposure, particularly on TV, than your programme will. It is up to you to make your approach just that little bit different so

A club rally start may lack some of the glamour of an international – but none of the enthusiasm.

that it gets attention. But don't go over-the-top with expensive over-designed glossy publications or by overstating what you are offering. Marketing men are not fools.

Should you use a sports agency? Not unless you have a well known name either from another sport or, say, show business. We've seen presentations from amateurs which are just as well presented as those from sponsorship agencies and frankly, as an unknown you are unlikely to get the best brains in the agency working on your account. In any case some agencies' 'percentages' might be as much as your sponsorship figure! Press on yourself.

If you do get a bite from your fishing for a sponsor and are invited to a meeting, go neatly dressed and properly prepared. Think beforehand about how your programme and the particular sponsor could be welded together. Do be prepared to sell yourself but don't give the impression that you are seeking charity. And don't assume anyone in the company knows the first thing about rallying – expect their eyes to glaze if you waffle on too long about Group N, Group A, etc.

If you manage to find sponsors, don't just take the money and do nothing.

If you want to keep sponsors you should:

● Ensure that the terms of your association are clearly written down before the programme starts so that there is no confusion or embarrassment during the season. Cover such things as what happens if you miss a planned rally for any reason.

● Send them results after every event.

● Send them press cuttings on a regular basis.

● Visit them at least once a month to keep them informed.

● Suggest ways in which their involvement could be expanded, such as by bringing customers to rallies, running competitions in conjunction with the local press and so on.

● Invite them to a test session. Perhaps let the decision maker at the company drive

A moment to savour for Kankkunen and Pironen. Even on the finish ramp the winners do not forget their sponsors when advertising caps will be donned before the flashbulbs start popping.

your car (slowly!); have his picture taken in the car.

- If your sponsors go to events make them feel part of your team.

- Never criticise sponsors or their products in public.

- Always present your car and team in a smart, clean condition.

- Half way through the season present your tentative plans for the following year so that decisions can be made in good time. Wise sponsors will see the sense of a long term link rather than a brief flirtation.

- Don't be extravagant. Spend sponsors' money wisely and make it a two-way exchange. If you give value for money you stand a chance of retaining sponsors for other years.

Finding sponsors will not be easy. You will need a professional, determined approach – and a lot of patience – but it *is* possible. Good luck! ■

CRYSTAL GAZING

We hope that reading this book will have encouraged you to take up rallying. If it has, you may wonder just what sort of future the sport has in store. Well we can't see too clearly into our crystal ball for all the sponsors' stickers on it, but really we need to look at the future in three steps: short, medium and long term.

In the *short term* the most immediate task is for the sport to fight harder for itself in the U.K., to get a proper share of facilities and access to stages. As people have more leisure, sport inevitably will have to be better co-ordinated – which means committees. This means that the sport must have proper representation on these committees. If not, we will be frozen out by bikers and hikers, as well as all sorts of other sports. The RACMSA will have to walk the corridors of power to see that the right representations are made to the right authorities at the right time.

Rallying is not a sport we need to be ashamed of; it is a sport which gives a lot of pleasure to a lot of people, either as competitors, officials or spectators: we should argue our case for facilities with vigour.

Sadly at the moment we don't help ourselves very much. Many motor clubs are far too parochial in their approach. There are too many clubs hovering around the 70 or so membership figure and there is far too little liaison between clubs. Clubs need to promote themselves and the sport better. How many clubs take an active part in their local community affairs so that they are seen to be responsible people, not just rock apes with noisy, smelly cars? Precious few. How many clubs work with local charities so that they get good media coverage in their area? Again precious few.

What has all this hectoring got to do with you, we hear you cry? After all, you probably bought the book as something of a beginner. Well, simply this – those of us who have been in the sport for some time haven't made too good a job of sorting things out. If you come in with a new and fresh approach, you may be able to help safeguard the future of rallying.

Stepping gracefully down from the pulpit, let us consider one or two other short term aspects. *Regulations should be made simpler.* Motorsport, including rallying, is far too complicated particularly compared with football, athletics and so on (which are often competing for the same sponsor's pot of gold, don't forget). Making the technical regulations simpler should help to prevent scrutineering problems and protests; it doesn't help the reputation of rallying if final results are not known until weeks after an event. When did you last go home not knowing the result of a football match? And what on earth must the layman make of nonsense like Group A and N? Probably nothing. How much better it would be for the sport's projection if they were called Standard and Development categories.

Costs must be kept down. If someone of eighteen wants to be a footballer he need spend little or nothing on equipment; he or she *could* be a tennis star at very little cost. If he wants to be a rally champion, somehow or other he has got to get behind the wheel of a car. The more we can do to make it easier for him the better. Let's see more 'one make' formulae, with rules designed to keep expenses to a minimum. It goes without saying that anyone caught cheating should then be slung out for a year. Even major manufacturers are beginning to bitch about costs. Tyres in particular are a cause for concern. On the opening day of the Lombard R.A.C. Rally (which consists of short stages) teams have been known to change wheels and tyres seven times, thus fitting 28 new tyres *for a total of 27 stage miles*! Lunacy? Of course, especially if you consider the attendant costs of vehicles, mechanics, tyre warmers and so on.

Safety will need constant vigilance. After a serious accident there tends to be a flurry of concern, followed sometimes by a relaxing of attention to this important area; we need to guard against this. Rallying is not *so* well established with the public or the media that it can necessarily withstand the impact of a major incident. The 200-off Group B category was abruptly cancelled for rallies after a tragedy and it is not unknown for events in some countries to be cancelled following a bad accident, even one in another country altogether. You see why we need to be vigilant? Watch almost any video on any rally and it is alarming to see spectators and even marshals standing in dangerous places.

Somehow we must make it impossible for an absolute beginner to enter a rally in a full-house works replica (perhaps via restrictor plates to limit engine power). No one would expect to leap into Formula One without experience. Why should they do so in rallying? One, or two simple power-to-experience formulae would give rallying the equivalent of the Formula Ford, F3, 3000; stepping stones into F1.

We cannot pretend that we expect road rallying to have a long-term future. The days of national championships and cut-throat competition have now gone forever, but there is still a place for road rallying as the best training ground for the disciplines of co-driving. In order to curb speeds, road rallies must become more navigational in nature and cars must be kept quiet and low-powered – maybe there should be a 1300cc limit? On this basis the sport can continue and can still be the starting point for the stars of tomorrow..

In the *medium term*, much depends on the Common market. Yes, really, because inevitably any legislation passed on the motor vehicle is going to affect rallying. In addition, concerns over dying forests have had an effect on rallies in some countries and such concerns are unlikely to go away.

Private tuners may find it increasingly difficult to get through legislation, which may leave manufacturers with a stranglehold on what is or isn't allowed.

We shall see an increasing shift to single stage events at the club level and there will still be letters in the enthusiasts' press calling for British roads to be closed for rallying. We are not optimistic.

One thing rallying has to face in the medium and short term; much tougher competition from other sports. In the relatively brief period between editions of this book, other sports have increased in prominence and therefore attracted sponsors, TV and spectators who might otherwise have turned to our beloved sport. This could be one reason why many clubs now face a shortage of marshals. Rallying will simply have to recognise that there is a wider world than just special stages, and will have to market and project itself accordingly.

Long term? Your crystal ball is as good as ours; it all depends on energy resources and green issues. Much as we all love rallying and much as we all shout about its benefits, we have to face facts. The facts are that if people are shivering under blankets because they have no oil for central heating, then there is no way we will be rallying. We'd be lynched if we tried. As we would if we tried to rally when there was violent opposition on environmental grounds.

It won't come to that. Man's love affair with mobility via the motor car is a deep and lasting one. Man's ingenuity and drive will therefore lead him to overcome any energy problems we may see looming in the distance. So if we still have transport, a select band will still want to go faster to test themselves (there is no sign that the human race is losing its healthy desire for excitement).

If man still wants to go fast, then there will still be races and rallies. Come to think of it the way some roads are being maintained at the moment, rallying will be more challenging because the roads will be rougher!

We make no attempt to forecast what means man will use to continue motoring. If we ever have electric cars then we will need a whole new breed of noise marshals, people to check that cars register at least a certain minimum noise level. If they don't the cars will be so quiet that spectators won't hear them coming, which will be dangerous!

To study the future, it is helpful to study the past. If you look back twenty-five years or so, rallying wasn't all that different then. You could find your way around quieter areas of the country today with the maps in use then and techniques with pace notes, servicing and so on have not advanced much since the early Sixties; some of the stars of the Seventies are still rallying, and rallying successfully (which is why there are such golden opportunities for a young person like you – they *must* retire sometime).

Overall we remain optimistic. Rallying should stay healthy until well into the next century. Have fun! ∎